Ordinary People as Monks & Mystics

Lifestyles for Spiritual Wholeness

NEW EDITION

Marsha Sinetar

PAULIST PRESS
New York/Mahwah, NJ

Cover design by Cynthia Dunne
Book design by Lynn Else

Library of Congress Cataloging-in-Publication Data

Sinetar, Marsha.
    Ordinary people as monks & mystics : lifestyles for spiritual
wholeness / Marsha Sinetar. — New ed.
    p. cm.
    Includes bibliographical references.
    ISBN 978–0–8091–4284–2 (alk. paper)
    1. Spiritual life—Christianity. I. Title. II. Title: Ordinary people as
monks and mystics.
    BV4501.3.S5845 2007
    248.2 2—dc22

                                                              2006101513

Published by Paulist Press
997 Macarthur Boulevard
Mahwah, New Jersey 07430

www.paulistpress.com

Printed and bound in the
United States of America

What readers are saying about
Ordinary People as Monks & Mystics...

"The book is terrific. It has given me—and I am sure many others—a lot to think about on what is really the one subject of ultimate importance—our place in creation and our relation to the Creator....a wonderful blend of the modern and the traditional."

"So much of what it says connects for me, as I'm in the position of being an extrovert who needs the social contact yet also needs the contemplative dimension in daily life."

"I am savoring it—read a few pages a day. *Ordinary People as Monks & Mystics* is a great help in understanding myself, and I feel more content in being 'my self'."

"Thanks for a whole book of positive thinking....Here are unsung heroes, monks and mystics who have much to share, a light to shine, and wisdom to spare...."

"...I'm sure this will not be the last time I turn to it. It's the kind of book that is both reassuring and challenging. Reassuring in that I agree with its description of 'wholeness'...challenging in that it gives the subject a completely new dimension. It defines an entirely new set of goals which I hope to move toward, however, slowly."

"I enjoyed reading *Ordinary People as Monks & Mystics*. I found it to be very uplifting."

"The book and the questionnaire fascinated me."

"The title attracted me immediately, and I was deeply engrossed in it from page one....I am a very ordinary person living a very ordinary life, and I appreciate the faith this book has in the ordinary. I also appreciate the encouragement it offers people in their ability to actualize themselves and the way it has removed the pressure of time from such a journey...."

"...an intimate forum of religious and spiritual thought."

"...extraordinary!"

"The book makes a great deal of sense to me from the inside out."

"This philosophical tour de force is enjoyable!—Though not speed reading!"

"I have passed along *Ordinary People as Monks & Mystics* to others as well as recommended it to many. I am hoping to have an opportunity to use the book in a class—or at least have it available for recommended reading."

"Marsha Sinetar is a marvelous teacher."

Other Books by Marsha Sinetar

Do What You Love, the Money Will Follow

Elegant Choices, Healing Choices

Living Happily Ever After

Developing a 21st-Century Mind

A Way Without Words

Reel Power: Spiritual Growth Through Film

Holy Work

The Mentor's Spirit

To Build the Life You Want, Create the Work You Love

Spiritual Intelligence

Sometimes, Enough Is Enough

Don't Call Me Old, I'm Just Awakening!

Illustrated Works:

Self-Esteem Is Just an Idea We Have About Ourselves
  (bilingual edition)

Why Can't Grownups Believe in Angels?

Contents

Dear Friend,

I saw your ad…and probably qualify for your project.

After moving south with my wife and stepchildren in 1980, I'm now a hermit in the woods. My wife died close to two years ago, and her sons subsequently moved out. I'm fifty-two, run a [small business] by myself and go "out" three times a week. There are no utilities here. I pump water, cut wood and take batteries out for recharging. I enjoy the solitude and try (not always effectively) to conduct my business as a service. I'm also committed to preserving my land as wilderness.

Sincerely,
Boxholder, Alabama.

Acknowledgments

※

It has been said that whoever finds what is "the good" and holds fast to it will become whole. This is such a simple truth, yet so difficult for most of us to carry out.

The people in this small, uncomplicated study are fine teachers about just this work: Each puts his or her own words and special mark upon the task of becoming whole. Yet, as a group, those in this book speak in a single voice about the costs and values of actualization—which is but another name for wholeness. By their life-examples and disclosures they show what actualization requires.

I've tried to quote each person as accurately as possible. Given the fact that, in writing a book, style and clarity must also be taken into account, in some cases I've edited their comments. To the best of my knowledge, I've kept their sentiments and intent intact.

Two people helped so much with the initial reading and editing of this material: to my neighbor and most talented friend, Patricia Ditzler, who read and edited the earliest chapters of this book and who so encouraged me along the way, I owe a tremendous debt of gratitude; to my project editor, Dianne Molvig, who manicured and organized each chapter, I say thank you. There is no way that someone with a work, writing and travel schedule like mine could have remained faithful to the requirements and enormous task of writing a book without the ongoing encouragement, optimism and support of such fine colleagues.

I must add a word of thanks to Georgia J. Mandakas Christo, my editor at Paulist Press, who made the process of putting the book together effective and smooth. I did not expect a long-distance editorial relationship to become a fast friendship. The whole experience turned out to be a happy surprise.

To each study participant, I express my deep thanks. For joining the study in the first place; for having had the trust and openness to answer my questions when I was but a stranger; for inviting me into their homes; for giving me such generous amounts of telephone time for follow-up conversations; for having had the faith that something positive and productive would come of our interviews; for writing me letters packed with self-disclosures of the most personal kind; for sending me their favorite scriptural and literary quotations and experiential wisdom—I am enormously touched and appreciative. All the participants' willingness to be truthful, their natural eagerness to confront and—where possible—resolve the deepest conflicts of life, their simple dignity in conveying the values, organizing priorities and needs of their life, made this study a joy for me.

Preface to the New Edition

❋

> Wherefore do ye spend money for that which is not
> bread? And your labor for that which satisfieth not?
> Hearken diligently unto me, and eat ye that which is
> good, and let your soul delight itself in fatness.
>   Isaiah 55:2, King James Version

"A rebel," Camus once noted, "is someone who says no." It appears that I'm always writing about, and for, a certain type of wholesome rebel. Some readers tell me it takes one to know one.

The interviews in this book introduced me to mature adults who took risks, albeit well-calculated ones, to affirm their radical sense of selfhood. That's wholesome rebellion. No one expresses any poetry of soul without it, as any true artist, life-lover and saint knows. Back in 1984, when my editors at Paulist Press and I originally met to discuss publishing this, my first, book, they warned me not to expect success. Even then I observed people everywhere voicing wholesome protest, starting to network for a higher quality of life and wanting their own life to be genuine and fulfilling. I thought then, more so now, that my small group of study participants mirrored the deepest longings of our collective heart to say yes and no in daily life, as if the details of existence mattered.

The following chapters explore key motifs of such positive protest as "ordinary," self-actualizing adults describe what motivates their quiet, responsible revolt. Make no mistake: these are not malcontents. They're not fighting the system as much as they are proactively expressing some sacred value of the core self. Here we find mature men and women refusing heartless roles in what seem practical ways: some keep their day jobs to support their family, simultaneously reinventing themselves; others quit and start small solo businesses. They all pay their bills. By and large, they're rising up against some aspect of a false self that whispers they can't fulfill their sensed, most noble purposes.

In varying degrees, those I've called "monks" and "mystics" are surrendering their socially programmed selves to the overarching, or *meta,* law of their being. We meet them as they put their subjective house in order. This means honoring their authentic selves. As author Joseph Chilton Pearce once wrote, here we meet people who are not so much grappling with the unknown as they are moving their *knowns* into their unknowns. This is a critical characteristic of self-actualizing men and women everywhere.

Then too, the "monks" seem to be reaching out for the sort of liberty Gandhi called *moksha*—emancipation from worldly attachment (Mohandas K. Gandhi, *All Men Are Brothers* [New York: Continuum, 1980], 166). They remind me of the CEOs I was working with then, in my corporate practice. Although seemingly secular, these executives set a new standard for focusing on their own enchantments, and not so much on what mattered to others.

The "mystics" are raising the bar of an in-depth spiritual encounter. For me, this encounter—and never dogma—constitutes true religious communion. In the minutia of daily living, mystics demonstrate their vivid understanding of that sanctified reality; the one Jesus promised would set us free. None of them follow celebrity gurus or quick-fix advice from talk radio or TV experts. They are *intuiting* their life's compulsory course corrections in ways that demonstrate the sane, less stressful lifestyles that we hear so much about today.

Since great, heaping numbers of us appear to be adrift in a sea of spiritual crisis—the crisis that, in a fortunate few, tends to precede real healing—it stands to reason that great, heaping numbers of us might profit from making similar little course corrections. First, however, we need the self-knowledge, the soundness of mind, and skill to say yes or no in favor of wholesome living. Apparently these capacities are hard to come by. Just look at our current workplace: I recently read that job stress costs American businesses three hundred billion dollars in absenteeism, accidents, workers' compensation and workplace violence; our nation spent over nine billion dollars in 1984 (when I wrote this book). By 1999, that sum had soared to over eleven billion dollars. On average, one million of us are absent from the workplace each day, while nearly half of all the U.S. workforce suffers from symptoms of burnout, and 60 percent of employee absences are due to psychological problems related to stress. It's believed that between 75 and 90 percent of all our visits to primary care physicians are stress related. (Duane Elgin, *Voluntary Simplicity*, rev. ed. [New York: HarperCollins, 1998.])

However, much like Groucho Marx quipped in *Monkey Business,* haven't too many of us worked ourselves up from nothing to a state of extreme poverty? Fortunately, the adults interviewed for this book reveal a radically different pattern, and the strength of that message is a universal, timeless encouragement to get real.

The study participants are lucid. They have a strong grip on their sanity—an enviable emotional stability that seems to let each shape his or her own life's course. Each one's encouragement comes as a living example of the good life. Perhaps that's why this book has been passed along from reader to reader for over twenty years.

Power, to paraphrase something Professor Carolyn Heilbrun once wrote, is the capacity to take one's place in the discourses that are critical to our life's action, to have our say and our part in the matter *matter.* It was always my intent to find fresh ways to talk about and to describe the most profound spiritual side of existence as an educator who hoped to teach and reach the interested about their highest craving for authentic, wholesome living. That longing for adult development is too often misunderstood and overlooked. In 1984, I was forming a language for that discourse, just starting to express intuitions that embraced my own growth.

Ultimately, I'm sharing ideas for spirituality intelligent, stable individuals who know which end is up. My readers include scores of trusted counselors, human resource professionals and members of the clergy to whom we turn when faced with inordinate stress or ambiguity. To understand these interviews, one needs to know oneself well enough to discern when it is or isn't the right time to establish some sort of trusted dialogue with a competent, trusted counselor. Usually it's time to get professional help when our nonconventional choices heighten fear, discomfort, anxiety or depression.

Be clear, this is not a book of advice about how to lead a "balanced" life or join the voluntary simplicity movement. It won't urge you to reduce credit card debt or encourage you to become a vegetarian. As the participants describe their innovative solutions, we get a sense that these solutions could elevate uncertainty and fly in the face of convention. However, nothing says the self-actualizing journey means quitting a job or moving to the woods or throwing out Gucci bags. To slavishly copy someone else's way of life is precisely what one does *not* do when cultivating mature authenticity. In review, I emphasize that the self-actualizing men and women interviewed for this study:

- know, or at least sense, who they are at their most noble, essential core;
- know, or at least sense, what they value in the highest, most elegant terms;
- possess at least enough trust—faith, confidence, intent— to suspend fear and anxiety over survival concerns; to inch into their unknowns and tolerate, if not actively invite, the small deaths that lead to a larger, more abundant life.

They may be in a minority, yet they're not alone.

The study participants reveal how they are rethinking, reshaping and frequently removing themselves from the orbit of convention. They are renewing outworn ideas and forms of work, striving, relating, homemaking; they are reflecting the irresistible charm of saying yes to life. Far from producing an incoherent hodge-podge of choices, they express a life movement that is elegant, spiritually intelligent and, as noted, universally valued.

These revelations possibly explain this book's grassroots popularity: Who among us does not want to be guided by life's affirmation and our own law of being? Who among us does not agree that no earthly influence has enough power to stop our own unfolding, provided we do our little bit of righteous choosing?

Initially, such choices may seem intensely specific and goal oriented, if often inarticulate and imbued with some fear. The early phases of self-actualizing sometimes remind me of Kafka's notion that it is far safer to live in chains than to be free. Eventually, we note the study participants relax into who they are, without inordinate anxiety or that constant craving to improve something—their love-life, their social or economic status. Eventually, we hear these adults sounding as if they've grown accustomed to their own true face, confident enough to shed outworn perspectives like caterpillars slough off old skin.

Today, twenty years after conducting these interviews, I sense that we need to do little more than choose each day, *this* day, to follow that still small voice that breathes, "This is the way, walk ye into it" (Isaiah 30:21 KJV).

Introduction

My bias is this: ordinary people can and do become whole. They can and do live in ways that express their highest most cherished values—values that also happen to be those shared, most prized universally throughout history. People who become whole consciously integrate inner and outer realities. This is a book about such individuals and the way they merge their inner truths with the demands of everyday living.

Ordinary people can and do inspire others into healthier, more mature choices and behaviors. They can live as good stewards in their communities, simultaneously protecting their unique way of being in the world—a way of being that may be so idiosyncratic as to contradict and confound the logical expectations and mind-sets of those they would serve.

Ordinary people can and do resolve these and other contradictions alone, without guidance from experts or advice from friends and family. Ordinary people are some of our best experts and teachers of what it means to be self-sufficient and what it means to lead virtuous, courageous lives. This book tells of such people, and it is for them—and for all who identify with them, who would be whole—that I write.

My research began several years ago when my own inclination and interest made me pull away from the way I saw most people living, in favor of a more solitary, silent, reflective life. Although it isn't my purpose to describe my life experience, every book is in some sense autobiographical. This one is no exception.

1

My research was driven by an intuition of what it means to be and become self-actualizing. I had—still have—an intense interest in the values of actualization and in the process itself. My day-to-day work is that of a corporate advisor and educator who, for several years, has been increasingly interested in the adult choices, lifestyles and development of self-realizing men and women. Both in my practice, where my clients often are purposeful, wholesome and actualizing, and in this research project, where the values of actualization are more sharply focused, I have felt that the healthiest adults have much to teach about what it means to be mature, generous, virtuous and even happy.

Self-actualization—that state of psychological wholeness or completeness, subjective health and authenticity—emerged as a psychology, and as an idea, from the inspirational work of scholars like Abraham Maslow. The phrase is now surrounded by much myth and commercialism. Some people believe that people cannot be actualized; that people are always in the process of becoming. Most self-help books, and even many psychological textbooks (directed at health-care professionals), treat the topic as if only a rare individual had self-actualizing tendencies. I see the matter differently. In later chapters I will discuss how actualization is our species' most natural aim.

But being actualized is not an end point. This is where I think the misunderstanding of the term has its roots. It is not a final or static destination at which a human being arrives, only to stop growing. It is a starting point, to my way of thinking, a birth as may have been meant in the biblical phrase "born again" of the converted, the one who finds wholeness of being, that is, through Christ. This conversion is so profound that, after it, life expresses itself through the individual in a completely revitalized and original manner, if often hard to understand. I should add that my observations show me that most people are self-actualiz*ing*, not actualized, and that, like Maslow, for the purposes of simplicity and ease of expression, most of the time I refer to people as actualizing. However, I'll add that, contrary to some, my hunch is that there are many more self-actualizing individuals around than we expect, and that it is a natural manifestation of healthy human development.

I believe the numbers grow yearly, and that this increase has socioeconomic ramifications. This is a subject I've written about in terms of its impact on the American workforce and management[1] and need not elaborate here. But I should mention that some completely ordinary self-challenges are likely to be misinterpreted as problems (e.g., the "mid-life crisis," which the media often interprets as a foolhardy, perhaps unnecessary, stage of life) by those who don't clearly recognize the issues of actualization when they see them.

It has been said that the inception of real emotional health occurs when individuals stop trying to get the world to meet their needs and wants, and begin seeking out ways to perform some needed and meaningful service for others. That seems like a good and practical starting point for the discussion at hand, since it allows us to view wholeness through an inner/outer filter of how people conduct their lives in the context of community. This is helpful for several reasons. First, actualization involves some measure of pulling back, away from others. By viewing the process of growth as having within it one *stage* in which people move away from at least some part of social custom, we better understand what is happening in our own lives when we make such moves. Later in the same progression, the actualizing ones begin to relate to the external world through fresh, truly generous perspectives. Ultimately they feel connected to others, eventually exhibiting a level of caring for others that can be called service or stewardship.

Stewardship, as we shall see, is always unique in the actualizing and may not conform to what society or family may expect. For one, environmental concerns may become hugely important.

For another, especially the mystic type, art, prayer or poetry may be the gift given to others. In all cases, there is, as one research subject said, "a wonderful set of emotions" received from giving to others, caring for others; so much so that in the psychologically whole, social action is probably revealed at its best. Throughout this book, I give concrete examples of how progressively healthy people are able to integrate their own needs, talents and values with those of others, the environment, the larger community. In doing this, they serve self-and-other in highly creative, useful and fulfilling ways.

This book explores two primary values of self-actualization, which I call "social transcendence" and "self-transcendence." These are characteristics that the actualizing possess in varying degrees. Although I have made little attempt to measure, it seems the greater the degree of each trait, the greater the degree of actualization. Neither of these terms is original; both have been explored as routes to human liberation in history's great literature, religion, art and philosophy. Perhaps such self-relinquishment was what Jesus of Nazareth was talking about when he said, "Those who find their life will lose it, and those who lose their life for my sake will find it" (Matt 10:39): both social and self-transcendence involve letting go of old secure ways; a dying to the old self; a move into unknown, unchartered territories of the self where we find larger life.

A cursory definition of social and self-transcendence may help at this point to clarify these terms. By social transcendence I mean emotional independence or detachment from societal influences, even from other people when necessary. I call the monk one who has detached emotionally from a known, familiar and comfortable way of life in order to embark on an uncharted inner journey. The monk responds to an inner call, reinterprets his or her basic way of being in the world—which might include reinterpreting how he relates to others, work, marriage, church or other organizations, and even includes a renewed self-definition and place in the scheme of things.

And I mean more: I use the term *monk* without reference to gender, material status, occupation or place of residence, and with full knowledge that some people I'd call monks would not and do not, in fact, call themselves "monks."

I simply needed a term that would embrace the one who, due to an inner prompting, turns from familiar, secure patterns of social custom, relationship and community life toward something altogether unknown. I needed a word that embraced the imagery of silence, dignity and obedience that automatically accompanies one who embarks upon an interior journey, whatever route that may take and whatever the cost.

By *self-transcendence* I mean having experienced, or experiencing in daily awareness, the mystical sense as classically described in poetry or religious literature. Maslow, for example, defined the peak experience as an "ecstatic moment" and as a "moment of rapture." He and others liken the experience to that of love. During these moments the self, the ego (one's separateness) disappears, melts, as the individual fuses experientially with the object(s) of perception: the cosmos or nature, work—especially when praying, playing or producing an object, working on a craft—sometimes even with another, as with a mother and child, although this is not the likeliest mystic fusion.

The great religious figures and saints were *mystics* as I use the term. The great artists and poets are as well, and they communicate their experiences through their work. I simply searched for, and found, a few ordinary people (i.e., nonsaints, although one never can know; not great figures in the way commonly meant) who nevertheless—like Dante, Blake, Whitman, Emerson, the Transcendentalists, Swedenborg, Holmes, Tennyson, St. Teresa, St. Paul and others—have perceived themselves to be a part of the whole and have experienced a radical transformation or mysterious union with another reality or with God. I did not seek out nor did I encourage interviews with those whose main interest was what Evelyn Underhill calls magic: the occult, astrology or other supernatural powers and psychic phenomena. My interest was and is purely in that elevated moral sense, intuitional mind and unitive consciousness described in the great scriptural, literary and poetic works of humankind.

Only a few of those I interviewed for this study are mystics, while several have had a mystical/peak experience and even are sensitive to the transformative power of that moment. I should also mention that while there is, in human terms, no neat split between people who are monks (i.e., socially transcendent) and those who are mystics (i.e., self-transcendent), I have divided this book into two parts that treat each type as if distinct from the other. Of course, mystics may live as if they were monks, and monks experience self-transcendence. However, monks may be highly legalistic, "organization men" (even those in monastic settings). Such rational types don't usually remember having had a transcendent experience and often lack empathy for those who do.

Of those I interviewed, enough spoke freely of their mystic sense and state of mind that I was moved to include their experiences and way of perceiving in this book. Unlike those I call monks who wouldn't call themselves that, mystics always seem to know that they are mystics.

Mystics are the ones who hunger and thirst after righteousness, as the Bible puts it, the ones who yearn for increased union with the other reality they themselves feel is the true reality that heals and makes all things new again. The mystics' spiritual yearning is their most distinctive trait, called by some a "deep and burning wound," because it propels them toward the transcendent nature of life much as a lover is drawn toward the object of love. The term *mystic* may also describe the slow and painful path of completion, a joining or a progression that involves being in the transcendent state. That progression should not be confused with psychological development. The latter involves self-understanding, self-acceptance and "personal" integration. The former involves self-forgetting, self-vanishing: the disappearance of the personal self into the universal, God, the Absolute, or the Transcendent aspect of reality, the Tao. Thus the term *self-transcendence* (with its emphasis on the small "s" in the word *self*, as opposed to *Self*, the higher aspect of the consciousness) is the letting go of egoistic interests.

I should say a word about methodology in the study itself and how I located the participants. There was nothing sophisticated about my methodology; quite the contrary—I communicated, pure and simple. I was willing to talk to anyone who felt they fit the characteristics listed in my ad. I first sent out a survey. Later, if the survey response proved interesting to me and if the other was willing, we scheduled a face-to-face interview or spoke by phone, especially if distance proved problematic.

My only screening device was people's initial letters to me. Only three of the thirty-some people who contacted me about the ad didn't seem to fit my criteria. Two of these sent initial postcards so illegible that I felt they'd have trouble answering the lengthy survey form. The third sent a five-page, emotion-packed, disorganized letter that rambled on about pets and the occult.

I wanted to communicate with men and women who had pulled away physically, as well as perceptually, from conventional life. Although I come across many actualizing individuals in the course of my professional practice, my feeling was that there is another, less traveled path and I hoped to find adults who could vividly represent social/self-transcendence for readers. I sought to interview adults who have had to be responsible for the consequences of their choices (thus the age specification on the ad). And to locate these self-actualizers I just listed several key qualities that actualizers possess, thinking that only someone with those attributes would respond favorably to the list.

Aims

My singlemost aim throughout the project was simply to communicate with individuals (a) who had entered what Thomas Merton calls "the wilderness" of their own interior journey, yet (b) who managed to stay connected to others in some positive, contributory way through their work or community/social activities and who (c) were drawn to the call of my ad for whatever reason. I felt it important to my research that each one in the study have a positive connection with society. This was essential for two reasons: First, I planned to concentrate on those who were functioning effectively in their communities and were contributive, even though they might be undergoing many changes. My thought was that the solutions of such functioning would be helpful to others who might be undergoing personal change, who might want to pull away, radically alter their lives, yet who needed, or desired, to stay connected to society in some viable way.

Secondly, I am aware of one danger of merely "pulling away": withdrawing with a tendency to get too inward, passive, self-absorbed. At best, such tendencies are the high points of contemplation, the "let-it-be" attitude of nondoing that we read about in mystic and also in Eastern literature. At worst, pulling away can signify inability to function at any time. It can be a red flag for a variety of problems—dullness, depression, ineptitude or hostilities. I recall, for example, when starting the study, that some friends heard of my search for study participants and told me of a man who lived as a hermit in the backwoods of northern California. "He's a poet," they said, and proceeded to describe the way in which he lived: barricaded in his small cabin with plenty of guns and ammunition to keep visitors and strangers away. That was not the kind of person I was looking for.

I hoped (through a simple dialogue process with actualizing adults who were constructively active in the world) to learn something about their worldview, their way of solving problems and creating meaning in life. My sense was that if they had the rich inner life I hoped they had, they would have something of value and elegance to teach others.

Organization

This book is organized into three parts. The first part focuses on monks: their characteristics and some, but certainly not all, variations of lifestyle that might be suitable for other socially transcendent individuals. The first part also presents patterns exhibited by the socially transcendent and provides interview comments to better illustrate the points being made. The second part deals with a definition, discussion and overview of the mystic state, and includes selected interview material to describe the characteristics presented. Part three is an exploration into the ways in which both social and self-transcendence are of value to subjective health and how both actualizing factors may promote actualizing itself.

Finally, I have no idea whether this material will add light to the field of spiritual psychology, the study of, to use Abraham Maslow's phrase, "the farther reaches" of the human spirit. This field is already brightly illumined by the writings of people such as R. M. Bucke, Evelyn Underhill, Abraham Maslow, and of course Thomas Merton, whose writings span theology, psychology, philosophy and poetry, and who has deeply influenced my own life and work. I do know that the prompting to write about this subject and to do the research itself comes directly from within, so I have answered the call, however elementary the result.

Marsha Sinetar, 1985

PART ONE
The Way of the Monk

1
Advancement to Wholeness

I have minimal possessions, no real ownership of anything much. No TV, for example. I read, and think, and
when I want to, I talk to friends. I'm self-entertaining,
for the most part. I'm living in a communal setting,
where everyone shares chores and works with one
another. I've dropped out of a professional career and
now am working as a carpenter.

                                   Carpenter, California

A youthful client once told me, "People are whole when
they have the guts to live out their convictions, when they can
face difficult situations and everyday choices in a way that hon-
ors what's inside them." Her spontaneous remarks hit far closer
to the mark of wholeness than we may think.

Wholeness exists to the extent individuals are conscious of
and receptive to their innermost self. The more aware and accepting people become of their inner images and motives, the more
they become healed. The Jungian analyst Gerhard Adler once
wrote that the words *whole, holy* and *heal* all contain a deep and
constant similarity; they all convey the idea that wholeness and
healing are related. With each of these elements, we become
enriched and gain the sort of subjective power that blesses us.
Moreover, the true purpose and meaning of each life is wholeness, that state my youthful client called "honoring what's inside
them." Advancing to wholeness is the true occupation of human
existence.

When we think about our own healthy growth we probably
consider two coexisting, equally necessary factors: (a) self-knowledge

13

(i.e., knowing who we are at the core and awakening to our values, needs and wants) and (b) the ability, perhaps I should say the will, to act out that real self in our lives.

"Know Thyself"

This close tie between knowing and doing may explain why many of us resist self-knowledge. Certainly it takes great courage to know ourselves as we essentially are, at root. That knowledge makes demands on us, demands not everyone wants to fulfill. For some of us, self-knowledge means letting go of the idealized image we think we "should" reflect. Living out the real self may mean scaling back, living unspectacular lives. For others, knowing the truth of their being could require stretching out into untried, frighteningly difficult arenas. Whatever the demand, when we know a thing to be true, then appropriate, responsive actions tend to follow naturally and reflexively.

The subsequent choices are often painful. Authentic living requires that we alter our programmed self-view and way of life. Or let go of favored habits, perhaps even favored relationships. Choices such as these can be made quite creatively and boldly when we know what's to be done. Knowing ourselves is by no means automatic. Except for the rare individual. For almost everyone, in order to arrive at the knowing part of the wholeness equation, courage and the will to know must become paired, cooperative traits. The fearful hold themselves in check, are stunted, even crippled—although their bodies may be perfectly formed. The longer fear persists, the more they feel stuck, passively unable to express what they need and know they want. In my corporate practice, I have observed such fear masking itself as anxiety, or as a disorderly, confused mind, incapable of coherent thought or solutions. Fear also masks itself as pseudo-stupidity, apathy, as an irritating niceness due to its artificial appeasing quality. Even poor judgment can be a symptom of not knowing: effectiveness and potency buried under a miscalculating mentality.

Paul Tillich's phrase "the courage to be" insightfully describes what we require to be whole. In his book of the same title, he reminds us that the self-affirming life requires will: the will to have more life and surpass ourselves. That sort of courage banishes everything cowardly and is the opposite of submissiveness to external gods. Rather it affirms that which is most alive within. It is the will that compels us to take on difficult, but perfectly natural, life battles. It allows us to tackle the kind of small deaths that open us up to ever larger life.

The death that belongs to life takes many forms. One of the most common forms of this death is sacrifice, the letting-go acts of what I call the *small* self: egoisms—petty, self-serving, self-interested. These tiny deaths are part of being born into the vital freedoms life offers. "Die and become," Goethe wrote. "Till thou hast learned this, Thou are but a dull guest on this dark planet."[1] We'll return repeatedly to the subject of sacrifice. It is key to the actualizing life: a universal law, if I might express it that way, for those of us who wish to express the truth of our being.

Finding out what we really want, having the courage to be, do and have what we desire, requires facing the enemy within. This is difficult work for nearly everyone, and the reason the will is an essential ally. To face our inner demons means confronting our obstacles and rejecting the world of appearances as we move toward whatever we apprehend has value—toward what our real self wants. That may mean going against the wishes of those we love and admire. It may mean leaving secure, comfortable ways of doing things to pursue something insecure and frightening. We may need to face our fears and hesitations, our desires for security, approval and rest—all natural objectives of the small self that craves guarantees, applause, care. Growing up means dealing with difficulties.

On Youthful Growth

Even children's fairy tales and mythology advance this central message of how to be fully human into the deepest consciousness of our species. Fairy tales teach young children how to be courageous amidst evil and obstacles. They learn what it means to stand up to their fears. They learn from the stories they hear, before learning to read, that tribulation is an integral part of growing up, that such effort is to be expected. Stories teach, and I am convinced all children want to learn, that wholesome growth invariably brings with it conflict, dangerous experiences, Goliaths to slay. But all this is frightening if only because it is new; the child (eventually the adult) doesn't know if he or she can master the situation.

Children learn that the currency for that self-development is courage, also faith. They learn that they must do battle with those conflicts instead of running away. The stories they love most teach these lessons, teach much needed virtues and attitudes for living fearlessly, triumphantly. When heroes and heroines stand up to bad wolves, mean witches, evil kings or monsters, they emerge victorious. Thus they obtain that cryptic blessing enabling them to "live happily ever after."

As children learn to identify their diverse emotions with the characters and elements of each story, they begin to understand what, within them, leads to ruin and what force leads to a successful, whole life.

Children also want to know "Who am I?" as they identify with storybook characters. Like adult philosophers, they intuitively search for stories to help them transition from childhood into adolescence, later into adulthood. They instinctively know that they'll be happy, strong and secure in the true sense, to the extent they can answer that most intimate "Who am I?" question and live out their answer in the real world of friends, grown-ups and practical reality. Children are simultaneously inward-turning and outer-directed. They learn early what it is going to take to handle life. But since they are young and relatively helpless they sometimes choose to act in ways designed to get them the approval and love they so desperately need. And this choice, although totally understandable, sets up patterns of behaviors and strategies that don't always permit expression of their best selves. Children who passively accept the criticism or abuse of a dominant parent, and who later find it difficult to believe in their own self-worth, illustrate an early strategy that ultimately thwarts self-expression.

Inherent in the double-edged, knowledge/action requirement of wholeness is yet another idea: there is a truth within the core self that yearns to be known. The expression of this truth makes one exist, be real, in her own eyes, ultimately in the eyes of others. The collective wisdom of humankind holds a deep abiding idea that there is, within each, some substantive truth waiting to be known, waiting to be expressed. When psychologists speak about people having an "authentic personality," they mean that these individuals manage to express what is most genuine, truthful and real about themselves—in other words, that they are genuine.

Nietzsche linked human virtue to a person's ability to put the true self consciously into each deed. In his essay "On Virtue" he writes, "...that your very Self be in your action, as the mother is in the child: let that be your formula of virtue."[2] German mystic Nicholas de Cusa was said to have imagined God telling us to be true to ourselves so he could be with us. Again and continually, the writings that would heal us, the teachings that would _adamantine =_

make us strong, noble and whole, tell us that growth, power and wholeness are obtained only through self-knowledge, truthful expression and the courage to act on what we know to be real within ourselves. The teachings that mankind values most suggest that were we to actuate ourselves through our choices and deeds, we would be worthy of receiving the blessings and attention of God himself.

From the earliest times, many who embarked upon this path achieved heroic, perhaps even saintly, status. Even if they were thought to be madmen or heretics in their day, history eventually rewarded them. Some who went their own way, listening to the voice within despite the tempting draw of a more secure, comfortable, conforming existence, ultimately received collective admiration.

What Makes Life Worth Living?

Sir Thomas More, to cite one example, who lost his life because he would not bless his king's marriage, was eventually acknowledged as a Christian saint. Of him, playwright Robert Bolt says:

Thomas More, as I wrote about him, became for me a man with an adamantine sense of his own self. He knew where he began and where he left off, what area of himself he could yield to the encroachments of his enemies, and what to the encroachments of those he loved....What first attracted me was a person who could not be accused of any incapacity for life, who indeed seized life in great variety and almost greedy quantities, and who nevertheless found something in himself without which life was valueless and when that was denied him was able to grasp his death.[3]

In the last scene of *A Man for All Seasons,* a commoner comes to center stage to talk to the townspeople (and, by this action, talks to the audience as well) after More's beheading. He asks the onlookers, "I'm breathing.... Are you breathing too? ...It's nice, isn't it? It isn't difficult to keep alive, friends just don't make trouble—or, if you must make trouble, make the sort of trouble that's expected."[4]

To find what makes our life worth living is risky business, for it means that once we know we must seek it. It also means that without it life will be valueless. More than just a few find their most valued selves despite the risk, although the majority seem to be (as in More's day) people who don't wish to make any trouble—not even the kind that's expected. The majority shrewdly stay dull to what in them is life and has meaning. A few brave souls, however, do look within and are so moved by what they find that they sacrifice, from then on, whatever is necessary to bring that self into being.

Anyone who answers the summons of the core self has a vocation, in the original sense of that word: "to be addressed by a voice." The clearest of vocations can, of course, be found in those who have a religious calling or who are driven to express some form of genius. But I believe that the word *vocation* should have a broader interpretation. Those who are called to find the law of their own being, for example, who answer that call obediently, even if hesitatingly, have a vocation. Those who sacrifice the things of this world, the conventional way of living or perceiving things, have a vocation. Anyone can be called—not just the religiously inclined or the great, gifted ones.

"Who Am I?"

Conscious assent to the inner summons and the subsequent alteration of life and worldview first requires a step back. That progressive sorting-out I call social transcendence. Social transcendence may develop spontaneously, as in the case of one woman who told me she had always known she was different, had always felt something within guiding her in one direction or another. Or it could begin as a decision in one's teens, as it did for a man of eighty-eight who said that when he was just a boy of fifteen he looked around at the other young boys in his community and at school, saw the way they were living, and decided right then that he would have something else, that there was more value within himself. He decided to hold himself to a stricter standard, to elevate his standard of living and make something out of his life as a whole.

Rewards of Social Transcendence

In order to know what within is true and of most value, as these sorts of insights come, the individual detaches experientially from the rules, customs, belief systems, conventions and various idols of the external world. Social transcendence answers this inner call, be it a physical response (such as moving out of one's parents' home, leaving a hometown or changing jobs, etc.) or an emotional detachment from social norms. Consider a woman, let's say, who decides not to marry, not to have children, even though she sees her friends doing that and knows that it's what her family expects her to do. Emotional detachment may be a sign that she has begun the process of actualization.

Social transcendence tends to be growth-motivated when the individual is becoming more of what he or she was born to be, more genuine. It is a wholesome response to an inner call that has as its goal self-knowledge and truthful self-expression rather than a fear-anxiety-motivated reaction to outer cues. While the socially transcendent may take conventional life lightly because they are growing more conscious of universally cherished, heartfelt values, their choices are not necessarily antisocial. On the surface it may appear as if these individuals are losing interest in traditional doings, but in the long run the self-actualizing develop a progressively cooperative, stewardly and morally concerned awareness better able to neatly balance selfish/selfless life as regards the world.

Autonomy

How interesting that Abraham Maslow acknowledged this phenomenon in a paper he presented in 1951: he reported that his healthiest subjects were independent, detached and self-governing. They tended to look within for their guiding values and for the rules by which they lived. He also observed their strong preference, even need, for privacy and their detachment from people in general. Maslow's healthiest subjects were superficially accepting of social customs, while in private they were quite casual, even humorously tolerant of them, not feeling these protocols were very important to them. They had the ability to fight convention when they thought it necessary, and judged things by their own subjective criteria. When they felt that something (usually about American culture, in the case of Maslow's study) was good, they accepted it. When they felt that something lacked value, they rejected it. For all these reasons, Maslow called such people autonomous.

He meant that these individuals were governed by the law of their own being, rather than by the rules of society. Lest we think that such people will lead themselves and us into anarchy, it is helpful to note that throughout his writings Maslow suggests that only the healthiest individuals—the most whole—are capable of making choices in a way that they select what is probably good for them and good for all. For example, "in these healthy people, we find duty and pleasure to be the same thing, as is also work and play, self-interest and altruism, individualism and selflessness.... Only to the self-disciplined and responsible can we say, 'Do as you will, and it will probably be all right.'"[5]

Universal Values

Others also have reassuring words about the values expressed by the self-actualizing. Psychotherapist Clark Moustakas identifies a host of ideals he calls "universal values" that, collectively, represent life, health and the consistently essential values of mankind: love, truth, freedom, beauty, justice, to name a few. These are the qualities that represent the good and that give individual life (as well as relational life) its meaning, depth and stability. Moustakas calls the individual "authentic" who is "genuinely present, and present in such a way that his freedom is used responsibly; growth of his self is rooted in genuine existence, in justice, and in truth."[6]

Moustakas links self-betrayal, the fall from authenticity, to a failure to stay with universal values. I am convinced that as we move into authentic, self-actuating relationships with ourselves and others, we live out "the good" in ways that inspire and effect the good for all. Only healthy individuals have the strength and will, for instance, to love their enemy, to do unto others as they would be done unto. Only in those who have established a link between the light of their integrity and their choices do we see expressed the will to obey what is known to be the good, the honest, the true.

Conversion of Manners

Social detachment involves a conversion of manners, to use a term from monastic literature, a term explored more fully in the next chapter. Once individuals have answered a vocational call, everything in life is absorbed into—perhaps I should say sacrificed to— this journey. Everything is given up (if gradually, incrementally and with resistance) so as to meet the requirements of that call. In other words, one undergoes a radical reinterpretation of day-to-day living, even, as we shall see, a radical reinterpretation of self. Yet this is always done in differing ways and degrees, depending on each and the situation encountered when the work begins.

As mentioned only superficially in the introductory remarks, social transcendence takes place within the context of *any* lifestyle. While I sought out people who had physically detached them-selves from urban and suburban living, the corporate clients I work with on an ongoing basis clearly are of the monk type. Their vocation, as it were, is business. They are, for example, gifted in finance or strategic planning, and as disciplined and committed to their call as, say, Trappist monks are to theirs.

While the degree of social transcendence may differ, and while the severity of sacrifice is as varied as the individuals them-selves, some patterns of letting go are shared by all who are called to any vocation:

- Sacrifice of collective opinion, custom, vanity, security, guarantees in favor of identifying and expressing the deepest values of one's life: love, truth, health, beauty, compassion, etcetera.

- Sacrifice of living unconsciously, of not knowing who one is or what is right in favor of bringing the law of one's being into existence through conscious expression.

- Sacrifice of direct and "safe" routes of accomplishment in favor of those that may be more demanding, risk-laden, ethical, illogical, unpopular, etcetera.

- Sacrifice of the individual's peculiar, risk-avoiding tendencies (e.g., withdrawal from conflict or avoidance of difficulty) in favor of reliability, commitment and responsibility in relationship to self-and-others.

Of course, the swing to the new perspective and conduct doesn't happen overnight. It takes many years. As one man of forty-eight admitted, having struggled to bring about some of these behaviors in his life for almost a decade:

When I realized what I had to do, I knew I was in for the work of my life. I knew it was going to take me years. I saw myself at the edge of the abyss, at the threshold of that which I didn't know how to be—yet wanted to be. But I felt that even if the odds were a million to one, I could make it. Even if it took the rest of my life, I wanted to try. For I saw that without making the effort, I really had no life, not one that mattered anyway. So I just made up my mind that however long it took, I would do the work.

2
The First Step

I need so very little to live on. Having "things" just interests me less and less. I sleep when I'm tired, and not much more than four hours per night. I wear khaki trousers to all events, with or without a jacket. All of what I wear appears to fit into a chest of drawers. I eat very little. Conversation is more important than radio, TV, movies, etcetera. I am a solitary person and I read a great deal.

Study participant and businessman, Pennsylvania

There are as many ways to answer the call to wholeness as there are people called. Therefore, it may help to see if we can find a pattern in the structure and organization of those who, for all intents and purposes, have pulled away from conventional life.

Those who enter a formal religious monastery find life organized in minute detail. Traditions, the rituals and philosophical tenets of their belief system, the very necessity of integrating one life with many lives in a smooth-running fashion, creates a structured, corporate environment with most major decisions taken care of by policies, customs, dietary practices and use of time. All the minor trivia of day-to-day living and worship are tightly organized for the monasterial citizen. The great religious traditions have given us examples of these organized approaches to the inward journey. Almost every major religion has had its group of devotees who withdrew from conventional life to live as disciples in the deepest way possible, within the context of their faith.

Monastic life and the organization that encouraged such a life precedes Christianity. In Hinduism, for example, isolated caves, mountaintops and ashrams have been home for the religious, either singly or in groups. Here they practice their arduous yogic and meditative prayers so as to experience *samahdi:* that state of superconscious awareness of identity with God. Zen Buddhists enter a monastery for much the same reason: to see and experience their highest reality, the truth of being, within the structure of the monastery.

The Universal Monk

However monasteries may differ in religious traditions, each structures life tightly for its residents so that they can attain basically a shared goal: union with God, as defined by them. In striving for that union, they retreat from worldly activity and life as others customarily live it. All increase their solitude, silence, orderliness of life. Thomas Merton once wrote that the monk is not defined by his task or by his usefulness. The monk lives in order to concern himself with life itself, not to exercise a specific function. This precept sums up the lives of all who would be monks: they respond to that within themselves which is life; they attempt, through each act, choice and habit to embody truth and love.

In Catholicism, the term for the practical adjustments and sacrifices by which monks alter daily life is "conversion of manners." Through a variety of vows and obediences, monks develop stability in their practice and in their faith. Vows like poverty and chastity, rules like silence and service alter a monk's conduct, interests, sensuality, even his freedom to come and go freely. All is subordinated to the authority of tradition, to elders, to God.

In the silence and simplicity of their lives, monks learn to listen to their persistent, interior voice of discontent. By abandoning worldly distractions, by assuming a conversion of manners, their newly structured life forces them into intimate and growing relationship with their inner "voice." Their absorption with this voice, their heightened listening powers, is not usually possible in the distracting environment of the world. Thus various vows cultivate and strengthen a deep posture of inner awareness.

Secular Conversion

By contrast, the secular, socially transcendent individual— or "monk"—lacks ready-made daily routine or like-minded others with whom to associate. There is no concrete blueprint for organizing a secular life dedicated to becoming more genuine. That involves having more time to think, reflect, study and commune with one's deepest self. Each necessarily designs his or her own structures.

As we will see, it is not just by taking formal vows or by living within the strict rules of a monastery that people break with conventional life. Sometimes their ability to detach from that life just happens as a perceptual shift, a lifting-out of the normal way of seeing and relating to traditional interpersonal/social reality. One man described that perceptual shift like this:

> I've had the ability to observe myself in society at large for a long time. I've seen myself constantly able to view things in the bigger picture. I know I spend more time conceptualizing about life in general, while at the same time seeing myself as an actor in the activity I'm watching. Your questions, for example, were easy for

me to answer because these are the kinds of large-issue questions that I've thought about for a long time. I'd say that what separates me from the norm is my ability to conceptualize in this way—to stand back and see things as whole, while continuing to observe myself.

Anyone who develops this critical, objective and conceptual sense in relation to society can, in the broadest sense, be called a monk. I agree with Merton: social movements such as the hippies, the civil rights movement, the peace movement, as well as individual interest in spiritual disciplines such as Yoga or Zen have aspects of conduct that can be called monastic. These social and individual tendencies imply a radical break with ordinary life and social patterns. Says Merton: "They have their asceticism, their 'discipline,' in the various kinds of sacrifices they make in order to 'break with their own past,' with their own normal milieu, with the society of parents, or with the social order with which they violently disagree....They represent an attitude toward the world which is analogous to that of the monk."[1]

However, such detachment with respect to conventional life has its problems. For one thing, a sense of meaninglessness can develop for the uninvolved, those who find themselves always onlookers. The need to create meaning (i.e., perhaps *new* ones when old ones prove pointless) increases as we pull back from engagements others find meaningful. Another practical concern relates to structuring daily life. Because a common goal of all those in this study was a desire to have more free time and fewer demands from trivial activities, people showed themselves capable of tremendous creativity: some were frugal in their way of meeting financial and time-management goals. Unlike the religious monk, those in secular life have no preset daily schedule. Also, they could need to locate their own practical solutions to a variety of problems: how to work while still preserving time for study, meditation or other activities, for example. This is a key concern for secular monks who usually are not financially independent and must continue to support themselves. Previous commitments to spouse, children, friends who might be dependent on them for economic or emotional support present other problems. Simplifying life becomes yet another issue to deal with; the socially transcendent usually want to carve out more time for reflection, study or inactivity—"nondoing" as in the Zen tradition.

Certainly each solves these puzzles in his or her own way. Yet strong similarities exist, enough to see as common patterns among study participants. Whatever the outer form of life, each lives in such a way as to become more conscious of the essential, core self. Some manage this by living alone; others divide time between two residences; still others systematically separate themselves from family and friends. The frugal and judicious use of time, money and other resources was another common motif. So was the continual defining and redefining of oneself in relation to the world.

Of Two Realities

I should mention at this point that the study participants seemed to be dealing with two types of reality and trying to integrate these. The first has been called the transpersonal (or superconscious, or true Self, or higher Self, in other words the depth aspects of wholeness). The second reality I would call consensus reality. Of course this involves the self in relation to others, the environment, the social order of things. Initially, as individuals desire to understand and deepen their bond with their transpersonal reality (i.e., all the various aspects of themselves: their subjective life, dream world, feelings, physiological tendencies, the unique demands of their physical or nervous systems, etc.), they pull back from the interpersonal sphere. Eventually, as we shall see, especially in the chapter that deals with the stewardship pattern, interpersonal reality changes, particularly for the socially transcendent. In the advanced, more mature actualizing individual we note relatedness to other-and-environment increases in a generous, caring way. At first, however, much like a child needs nurturing from its parent, these individuals need to be self-nurturing; this is when detachment takes place and may help that sheltering movement.

The withdrawal stage can last many years as transpersonal reality gets clarified and strengthened. Not only do individuals think differently about themselves, but they also begin to view themselves, experience themselves, as acting differently. Their choices and acts start to honor their clarified and most cherished values. It is as if a higher *faculty* of the self emerges into being through awareness, will, choices and acts. This aspect of self energizes one's ability to know and act on what is known to be true.

Obedience sums up the altered way of knowing and behaving and clarifies a cluster of changes depicting this first phase of social/self transcendence. "Obedience" means that we will that which accomplishes our highest objectives. Obedience is submitting to authority. Of course, within the framework of the traditional monk's solution (i.e., residing in and membership in a cloistered, religious community), obedience to authority is more easily defined, observed and understood. However, for the secular sort of socially transcendent there isn't someone superior, "out there" (i.e., in the home, organization, community or church) telling one what to do. Rather, it is we ourselves who desire something more, desire the goals of the inner self. Now, we learn to listen carefully to the inner authority as a way of saving our integrity, our very lives. Of this goal, one man said, "My work, as I see it now, is just to hear what the Self is, hear what it wants me to do. I would also say that a person's growth in this way, the level

of receptivity to the directives of one's own being, is the most ✦
important contribution we can make to the world, because these
directives are always healing."

"Experiential Anarchy"

Thus, for both the socially and self-transcendent, authority
rests in the truth, or law, of the higher Self. This poses problems
since such a law is ineffable, often just a subjective sense or inner
stirring, and in the initial phases is also a changeable sense. The
still, small voice, to be sure, but faint and tinged with conflicting
emotions. The phrase used by psychiatrist R. D. Laing, "experiential anarchy," comes to mind for describing the earliest stages
of trying to locate continuity in this internal authority.

One woman wrote to me asking to join the research group.
She epitomizes the inner anarchy that makes specific directives so
hard to pin down and comprehend. As she wrote:

I filled out your questionnaire yesterday, put it in the
envelope, sealed it, and then ripped open the envelope
and made additions and corrections, was about to go
to sleep, ripped it open again, made some more additions, slashed out a bunch of stuff and sealed it up
again. This morning I got up, opened it again, read it
over and threw it in the fire. I had to conclude that I'm
really not the type of individual you're looking for.
You see, I'm doing what I'm doing, but I'm not sure
why. I uprooted myself from the east coast last year
when my youngest son (of five children) was accepted
at college, and I could finally do what I wanted to do:
quit my boring job and go to the California coast,
which I've always loved, to live by myself for the first

> time in my life.... I've been doing this for a year.... As
> far as declaring a philosophy of life, that really threw
> me....I simply am unable to come to any definitive
> conclusions.

Because I sensed that she was in the early throes of pulling
back—an often disjointed, incoherent, and disturbingly noncon-
forming season, I wrote her a note saying just that. Soon I
received another letter:

> You're right. I'm on an incoherent journey fostered by
> faith and trust. In fact, I think my entire life could be
> described that way. I think what upset me so much
> about your questionnaire was that I was forced to
> admit this to myself. When stable people ask me ques-
> tions about my background I have a regular spiel
> which I rattle off, putting everything into a cohesive
> pattern. I've done this so often that I believed it
> myself. Psychologically sound people, I was taught,
> have structure and purpose. They know what they're
> doing. The only people who know me as I really am
> are my children. I can be thoroughly honest with them
> because I know they'll love me no matter what I do. I
> knew you were looking for true responses to your
> questions, and I couldn't do it because I had never
> done it before. Strange.

Her remarks are repeated in one way or another by those in
the study who find themselves in hard-to-understand life situations, especially in the first stages of their actualizing progression.

Fortunately, as time passes the demands of the higher Self
are easier to hear. This is especially true as life becomes well
ordered and simplified. The general rule is this: as our external
life gets simplified and less distracted, our inner life is strength-

ened and refined. If anything, pulling away from conventional life (if withdrawing is rooted in our sincere desire to be authentic) forces us to dignify our struggle to reveal our true self. By hearing, and obeying, the demand to make life-adjustments, we gain strength to grow. In fact, as will be described in the next chapter, many capacities grow along with self-trust and our bond to Self. With each correction, we give more power to the deeper Self, hear its voice with more clarity, feel more purpose to life.

One man said of his increased clarity of what was required:

> I was burdened by the weight of an inner vision of myself as an ignorant man, cowardly and afraid. I was nearly broken by the knowledge that I had to change my life myself, that I alone had to develop a closer affinity to God—that is to say, to Self, to Life, to the Tao, the Great Unnameable. I had to set it up so that that an affinity could develop. My work was well defined once that awareness surfaced.

Impetus for Growth

A first impetus for spiritual growth is a sense that something in one's customary way of living doesn't work, isn't health-promoting, isn't life-supporting. This initial awareness is experienced variously and at different times. It is usual even in the general population. What is unusual is that the socially transcendent do something: they alter their lives, as a result of their enhanced awareness, so as to further the development of the individual they sense they could be. Some people said they wanted time to sort things out. Still others described how marital problems or some disillusionment at home, at work or with world concerns sparked the initial awareness. Whatever the stimulus, that special light which comes with the knowledge that they must change helped people see things differently, and identify specifically what actions to take as next steps in their own development.

All those I spoke to had an intimate realization that propelled them to take the first step in pulling away from mainstream living. One bright and sensitive man said:

> In 1970 I saw a copy of the *Whole Earth Catalogue,* and it presented a whole new realm of possibilities to me. I saw a picture of the earth, riding in its finite little orb. That's what influenced me to pull away from the way in which others around me were living. The underlying philosophy that we have to take care of this fragile little planet was a challenge to my life. It made sense, and from then on I had the desire to figure out a lifestyle for myself that was consistent with that in every detail.

Another, a woman, reported something quite different. She and her husband both realized at about the same time that they needed to improve the quality of their daily lives, and that they wanted to increase the time they spent together. "We wanted better, more natural surroundings, fresh air and water. I need trees, hills, greater independence, more natural sights, sounds, and smells. I want to grow my own food. I want to learn as long as I live, and this new life we've designed is a way of fulfilling those needs. For my husband, our move was imperative since his health demanded it."

A young man, a former Olympic athlete, said of his urban life, "I found living in the city all week was unproductive. It sapped my strength in a way. I needed time out, time alone, time to reflect in a more solitary way what to do with my life. I needed more silent surroundings. I wanted to get away from the demands of my wife's career."

Discerning Necessary Adjustments

All these people share an ability to discern what they need and make appropriate life adjustments to accommodate those needs. All intuitively and specifically knew what elements to alter in life in order to live more honestly. It is as if some new faculty or power develops—a critical thinking/observing faculty that allows them to watch, editorialize and know concretely what to do in their day-to-day living in order to be authentic and whole.

For a few, this awakening, if I may call our detached—impersonal—perception by that name, came early in life. For others, the feeling gradually grew: that something more was necessary in order for meaning, purpose and wholeness to develop. One man in his seventies reported making the break with conventional living in midlife: He had wanted to live in a way that permitted him to become more God-centered. "I pulled away from the world through a desire to have more time for study, meditation, and prayer, and to search for a less violent way of life," he said.

A woman in her sixties said she knew early in life what she needed:

As a very young woman, I found myself able to extricate myself from some inordinately tough situations. I knew I was my own person, that I deserved to live in my own way. I felt myself become more secure within during those early days, and with this security came further detachment. I trusted my judgment about things and realized that my own unique perceptions were valid for me—valid enough for me to act on. These would provide me with the directions I'd need all my life.

Of Types and Traits

I should add a few words about the type of individual I sought for my study. As mentioned briefly in the introduction, my ad requested volunteers. I placed the ad in rural newspapers and in one national journal that reaches both urban and rural readers. Most of those in my study were either self-employed or retired. Only a few were financially affluent. Hence almost all had to be ingenious in finding a way to earn money to support themselves while taking some time off to think, reflect, live in sparsely populated communities. Some worked part-time. Some lived on nearly nothing; two participants volunteered the information that they lived on less than five thousand dollars per year. Another, a young woman, hinted that she lived on very little but didn't say how much. In no case did I ask people how much they earned, nor did I ask their ages. Many were uncomfortable with the latter, saw it as an omission and asked me why I didn't ask. When I replied that my ad simply sought people over thirty-five years of age and that age in and of itself didn't mean anything for this study (or perhaps I should add that it means little to me, as do other categories into which social scientists like to slot people), they seemed satisfied. Several men worked as carpenters, lived in cabins they had built themselves (or in cooperative communities in which everyone pooled their resources, lived very simply and rented cabins very inexpensively). Some worked sometimes, saved up their money, then took time off for rest and contemplation.

Whatever their financial situations, whatever the timing of their impetus for growth, the desire to think, study and reflect more and the yearning to pray or choose authentic lifestyles, say, by living in more natural, life-supporting settings repeatedly surfaced as participants' *known* goals. Their superordinate aspiration seemed the same: obedience to the law of their own, higher nature.

3
Practical Considerations

Being alone is very helpful and ordering to me. My desk, for example, is a symbolic way for me to organize my life. I clear it as a way of structuring myself. I live simply, without electricity, flush toilet, hot water, or recent model car. I have not had offspring, or done the usual family thing. My main work is helping improve the world and serving people.

Study participant and environmentalist, California

To obey the wholesome inner authority, we must devise practical, day-to-day routines that restructure our lives. There are obligations to meet, regardless of our individual financial situation. One may have plenty of money, but business interests to manage. Another may have children or a spouse to support emotionally and in other ways. Yet another may be retired with enough money and freedom to do as he or she pleases, but with health problems that constrict freedom. Each one in this study was different; each had a unique set of challenges to meet in order to create a new life. However, common threads were apparent.

Everyone said they now used money and other resources (e.g., food, transportation vehicles, community services) more wisely. I recall an interview with one man, of considerable means and financial security, who was surprised to hear that not everyone in the study was affluent. He had assumed, as many do, that in order to have the courage and ability to take on the so-called "higher" needs of development, people had to be financially secure. In fact, that doesn't seem to be the case. People have to feel *secure* before facing the work, but then that is another story.

To carve out a unique, meaningful life high self-esteem must exist: that strong underpinning of self-trust and self-worth that says, "I can do this if I really put my mind to it." Or, "Even when I don't know what to do in a situation, I know I'll be able to figure out what to do eventually." A bit of this quality involves self-respect and must be present in all who would tackle the hard battles of life. But just a little is all that's required. Taking on life's battles fuels self-esteem and self-respect, even when the battles themselves are lost. It is enough for us just to know we are willing to stand up and fight for something we believe in, value or care about. Having said that, I should add that everyone in the study was quite frugal with money: both those who had little and those who had a lot.

Time As Life

Time, not money, seemed the most coveted element for the revised life. This was especially true for those who were still working or who had spent many years working at an eight-to-five job and hadn't yet integrated work into the "work is play" scenario and tasks of the more well-developed self-actualizing people. The work-as-play attitude, as we shall see, is simply that balanced, constructive solution that comes as we do what we enjoy or are most naturally suited for. We get pleasure out of day-to-day tasks because these are the intrinsic expressions of our unfolding (as opposed to externally imposed tasks derived from doing work we feel we "should" do).

To claim more time for personal use, people scaled down their involvement with things and with obligatory but perhaps unsatisfying social activities. In this way they enhanced their ability to protect themselves from whatever they didn't wish to do. The objective is summed up nicely by what author-researcher

Duane Elgin calls voluntary simplicity. In his book of the same name, Elgin describes a way of life that is outwardly simple and inwardly rich and makes a strong sociological and environmental case for such a lifestyle. My impression is that all of the study subjects designed such a life for themselves.

One woman said:

> I've simplified my life so that I'll have time for the things I really want to do: I want to think, to read, to walk more. I want time for rewarding encounters with others. Simplifying outer things lets me order my interior life. I now spend a good deal of every day walking in the woods, making pottery, gardening and writing. I'm more clear-minded, and I believe I'm growing into a better, more responsible, even a nicer person.

Eager to share his new discovery, one man said:

> I've pared down my life incredibly. When I left my full-time involvement with a business venture, I vowed that I'd never work for anyone else again. I wanted more time to do what I knew to be important to me. I told myself it would be OK to work part-time, and that's exactly what I've arranged. This works for me because I'm involved in a structured setting, with definite hours three days a week, which I need. I've never had so much free time on my hands before. Then, the rest of the week, I keep entirely to myself, to use as I please. As it turns out, I've chosen to get up early, regardless of the day, go to sleep early too. I don't want to waste the time sleeping or watching television. I eat very simply, and I've given or thrown away most of the possessions that were just gathering dust.

Describing her life in yet another way, a woman from the Midwest said:

> My routine is stable. I don't do anything that seems pointless or boring. I don't waste money or time on things I don't need. I've separated myself from the way other people do things in that I'm not a joiner. I don't drink or smoke or take drugs. I read, think and write more than I believe most people do. I'd guess I give away more money than average. It goes to my church or to my children who are still young and struggling. What I give is peanuts since my income isn't large. Yet, I always have extra. I don't yearn for expensive things. And I always have enough to spend, save or just give away.

A sculptor, deeply absorbed in a new direction his pottery was taking, asked to be "excused" from *filling* out the rather lengthy research questionnaire. Instead, he requested an in-person interview to be held after his normal working day. "I just don't wish to give that much prime time to writing out these answers," he said, "since writing doesn't come too easily for me. But I'm sure I can tell you what you need to know in person if you can manage to interview me in the evening when my mind is not absorbed with my work."

Married people in the study reported many innovative ways to deal with individual needs for solitude, privacy and growing desire to alter social activity. In some cases, couples intentionally separated during the workweek and spent weekends together. In other cases, guest houses and separate quarters were established to give each other privacy and time alone. In most cases, marriage didn't end just because one or both parties wanted solitude. This seemed particularly evident in those relationships where both

people are reflective, quiet types who crave the same developmental results.

One married woman described her solution for obtaining
quiet time as follows:

> I use time each day when my husband is away from
> the house to sit quietly. This turns out to be quite a lot
> of time, about three hours or more usually. When he's
> home, it's still easy to spend time exactly as I want to:
> thinking, reading, contemplating. He's quiet too, and
> he wants time for just about the same things. He
> remains in his study, which is rather large and is
> almost like a separate apartment. I sit here in the din-
> ing room and look at the ocean for long stretches of
> time. My thoughts are usually on spiritual subjects
> now, not on community matters or on gossip. That's
> just not the current flow of thoughts I have these days.
> When there's another person in the house, I go into
> my bedroom and shut the door. I really don't like hav-
> ing houseguests any more. We've cut way back on
> that. We've even pulled away from our children, and I
> believe they're pleased to see us as self-sufficient adults
> with a life of our own. Somehow when we do get
> together our relationship is stronger.

"I have a good marriage," disclosed another woman, a wife
and mother of two children whose husband lived and worked in
another city for four days of the week. She went on to explain:

> For the last fifteen years, my husband and I have cho-
> sen to live apart during a portion of the week. We met
> in high school, and it was love at first sight. At least it
> was for me. For him, it was bewilderment. We dated
> until our early twenties, got married, had a daughter a

year and a half later and soon decided we wanted to move out of Los Angeles. So we bought a camper, and for almost a year lived in that camper, the two of us, our daughter and a dog. Our second child was conceived in that camper. I must say we both enjoyed every bit of that travel experience, and we'll return to that way of life when we retire. But now we have different requirements.

From Monday through Thursday, my husband lives in San Francisco where he works. I stay here with the children. That way he gets to do the things he wants without my having to do them, and I do what I want. I credit our strong marriage to this arrangement. Even my son has told me that all he hears at school is how the parents of his friends argue. "Mom, you and Dad never fight," he told me last week. It really felt great to know our son realizes we have something special.

One man characterized himself as highly competitive. He said he loved structure, describing his marital arrangement thusly: he takes two days a week to stay at his rural retreat home. He explained:

I wanted to uncouple myself from the demands of my wife's work, and it turned out that this solution worked for her too. I suppose you could even say we've switched roles. My wife is a physician who gets up before dawn. By five in the morning, she's out jogging with the dog. I don't see her until eight at night, and by then I've fixed dinner. I take care of the day-to-day decisions so that she doesn't have to. I even buy her clothes, and I think I do it pretty well, actually, because I have good taste. We enjoy having uninterrupted time to ourselves to read, think, reflect, so we

separate during a part of the week. I also have to structure the rest of my time pretty carefully because of my
time away from home, and that makes me very purposeful. I don't like my time frivolously taken up by
phone conversations or social things, even though of
course I do all of that. It's just that by slicing out a
piece of the week for myself, I'm able to do less of the
trivial things and more of what I consider essential.

Honoring What Matters

Almost all, married or unmarried, with children or without,
said they wanted to do what was important to them, even if it
meant others might think them selfish. Many realized that by pre- ✗
serving their strength and by cultivating their new sense of purpose, they would, in the long run, be better equipped to serve
others. Theirs is a tough love. As one woman, a wife and a mother
of two grown children, put it, "I feel that a person who says 'yes'
to all requests becomes scattered. I simply cannot satisfy those I
would serve if I'm pulled in all directions at once. So, what looks
like selfishness to some is at the root a selfless act."

As described in the last chapter, creating the new life
demands obedience. The secular monk is obedient to an *inner* ✗
call. In order to penetrate a larger truth, the transpersonal or spiritual reality, and give life meaning we may ultimately surrender
comfortable ways of doing things, our habitual response to life.
Perhaps most difficult is the matter of letting go of what others
think, or of the approval and even the love of others. Many in the
study spoke, often with poignant and lingering sadness, of parents, ex-spouses or friends who couldn't accept them in their
newly chosen lives. They missed those they loved, with whom
they could no longer communicate.

"My brother," explained one young man who quit school after high school and was working on and off as a carpenter, "is a very successful businessman, extremely involved with making money. He cannot understand why I live like this; it makes no sense to him, and of course most of the time I don't understand it myself, so it's hard for me to explain it. It's not a logical thing at all, and when I feel myself having to justify myself I pull back even more."

A young woman, whose father is a chemical engineer, lost her mother while still in college. She decided after college that she wanted to live in a rural area. She moved with a boyfriend to California. First she found a job as a waitress, saving her money diligently. Next she found some acreage overlooking the ocean, purchased that and finally built her own home, alone. Instead of acknowledging her actions as an achievement, her father withdrew.

"My father still wishes I would live out the American Dream," she says. "You know, marry, have kids, live in the suburbs. He can't understand my life. In fact, I think it makes him uncomfortable. He did come to visit me once, with his new wife. I was really looking forward to their visit and prepared for it, thinking they'd stay a few days. I mean, they did drive all the way out from the East Coast. But they came in, looked around at my little cabin, and I could see it was a strain for them to imagine my living here. They stayed for lunch and then left. I've felt badly about it, but there's nothing I'm going to do differently. I can't *not* live this way. I've always felt I <u>had to be true to myself</u>, and I act on that regardless of the consequences."

A woman in her sixties described her alienation from community norms:

> I live in a small town, and my family has always belonged to the same church. You have to understand that in this town, which epitomizes small-town southern…culture, people know about your business, and

they have a comment about everything. My family always belonged to a certain church, and so did I, and so did my six children. But in the 1960s I began to realize that the church was avoiding its responsibilities in the civil rights area. It seemed to me that the Christian position was not being taken by the church; at least that's how I saw it. Of course such matters are very personal. For my part, I could not in good conscience continue going to and supporting a church that didn't meet my criteria for Christian conduct. So I formally withdrew myself and my children from membership in that church. I'm not sure if you realize what it means in a small, southern town to do that. The action I took required all the courage I had. As I look back on it now I see that what I did made me grow in my own eyes. But living through that decision, and my subsequent actions, was one of the hardest things I've ever done.

Battling the Goliaths

Sometimes decisions like these, or others that involve a totally different set of circumstances and choices, look as though individuals may not be meeting their social or family responsibilities. For example, those who quit secure and promising careers in order to locate more satisfying, truthful work might be viewed as laggards, as unambitious, as irresponsible. As we have seen, family and friends can be rejecting when they don't understand (or cannot accept) the changes they observe. In a very real way that rejection can be frightening for individuals undergoing and engineering such changes. Were it not for some inward sense that change must be made they would probably not find the courage to make it. This observation underscores the importance of developing our will. German mystic Meister Eckhart reminds us that love has its being only in our will: "The man who has more will, he also has more love."[1] As we cultivate love for the Self, we simultaneously find the will to do what seems most difficult.

Many study respondents spoke of fears. These cropped up when grappling with unknown situations, lack of money, insecurity and disapproval of family and friends. Said one, "I have to say I feel an absence of integration when faced with uncertain conditions, as opposed to greeting my unknowns with more faith, more confidence. Of course, I do greet the unknown and do continue along this path. But I don't mind telling you that I get scared along the way."

Another said, "I've had to face the things which I've been afraid of most, my own abyss, if I can put it that way. But knowing what I was, knowing what I had to do, I realized that even if there was only one chance in a million that I could make it, I'd have to give it a try. There was no life for me otherwise."

The youngest person in the study, a woman of twenty-seven and a single mother living in a remote region of Nova Scotia, described battling insecurity:

> I've made a commitment to live by and work with my creative energy, pursuing a spiritual path. This is how I want my life to be…but I'd have to say I'm not secure in all of this. I feel as if this is my home in the "wilderness," my "desert," and so I just have faith in this process. Sometimes, though, I feel very vulnerable. I try to search inwardly for guidance, try to be sensitive to what I'm led to do. I'm not as good as this sounds, not always successful or disciplined, so I must stress the 'try' part of my answer. I came here because I love the beauty, the silence, the depth of where I live. I want to go deeper—I'm breaking new ground, alone.

Safety vs. Exploration

Exploration is a less important need than that of safety. We know, for example, that only one who feels inwardly confident, who has a certain degree of faith in his or her ability to meet the unknown, can venture forth. The two individuals quoted above, for example, are not affluent. The young woman from Nova Scotia organized a day school to support her young child and herself. The man who said he feels a lack of integration when he faces the unknown is currently working as a maintenance man for a development company that he doesn't really like. This type of exploration takes special skills, skills that come with the greater bonding to and trust of the Self.

One of those I interviewed—the sculptor who asked to have an interview rather than responding to the written questionnaire—said this about his self-trust:

I never pull an answer out of myself. It just comes as I have the need. The need to know something prompts the response from within. If I have a need, I have a sense of confidence in myself that I can fill that need. That's the way I communicate with myself—the need produces the answers. I trust myself...my self-talk is supportive. It's easy for me to love myself. I'm really quite a good person, even though I suppose I have my flaws. I respond as honestly as I can to situations. I don't have a lot of anger or prejudices. I've never intentionally hurt anyone, and I've experienced more difficulty than most people and survived it. I suppose that's why I trust myself.

The ability to confront conflicts and fears, to acknowledge our longing for security, for roots or unending love and approval,

yet—at the same time—to remain unswervingly fixed on an insecure path because we sense it to be *our* right path is, to my way
of thinking, heroic. *This* takes the courage to be. Thomas Merton
says of the monk who confronts his own challenges squarely,
"The paradox that one must face, if he really takes the truth seriously, is the pragmatic fact that sincerity means insecurity."[2]

Actualization As Sacrifice

Only the actualizing can sustain the weight of freedom,
even to make a truly free choice. To live in such a way that we
yield up anything that interferes with the truth of our being is an
entirely different way of life than is customary for the average person. Yet actualizing people demonstrate the ability to choose the
more truthful option in many tangible daily choices, as we have
seen in the examples given in this chapter. Repeatedly, the actualizing act out of a detached view of society—and often out of a
more objective view of self—even when those actions create discomfort, fears and unpopular outcomes. Again and again, the
actualizing adult sacrifices short-term security for long-term integration and truthful expression of life.

Ultimately, of course, what is sacrificed is one's separateness,
the "personal," small self. A great paradox of this developmental
route is that as we become more distinctive, original, perhaps
more narrowly idiosyncratic, we express a larger worldview, a
more unified perspective and greater universality. Almost all
those in the study commented on one fact: although they started
their journey by drawing back (into themselves), they found
themselves growing "out," back toward others in more contributive, expansive, supportive ways. The artists in the group wanted
to create and to share their creations with others. The peace activ-

ities became more community minded. A financial advisor expressed it this way:

> I feel the need to move out of my quiet, private, rather independent shell to work more closely with others. I feel a desire to teach more, extend myself. I don't know why I'm doing this since it's quite inconvenient, and I'm pushing myself out of my areas of comfort. It's not logical, because much of what I find myself doing is irritating to me: more crowds, more traffic jams, a tighter schedule. But I feel a need to do it anyway.

Our next chapter examines the pull of that stewardship pattern more thoroughly. Suffice it to say at this point that as actualization develops, individuals know themselves to be a part of an integrated world. They desire to function effectively and responsibly as a part of that whole. This motivational thrust—what Maslow termed "metamotivation"—is entirely different from participating in work or community projects because others expect it, or because it aggrandizes oneself.

Practical Reorientations

In review, we see just a few tangible considerations faced by the socially transcendent: Out of a self-imposed ordeal comes new life-meaning, a revitalized mode of being in the world and a cluster of aptitudes or skills that allows individuals to venture forth in varying degrees, as mature, interrelated members of society. Among many capacities that appear to develop, the following seem particularly worth mentioning:

• The ability to reinterpret oneself more truthfully in the context of a whole worldview: individuals alter their way of seeing themselves, the way they relate to others, work and community. They know and live out their values, with or without the approval of others, and begin to integrate inner and outer aspects of their lives in a consistent manner.

• The ability to manage resources—time, money, community services and such creatively and efficiently. The individual starts to control the various resources of life rather than experiencing the effect of them.

• The ability to release conventional pressures to achieve, earn material goods, status symbols in favor of more intrinsically meaningful things, activities and goals. This renunciation, as we have seen, encompasses a wide range of attitudes and beliefs and entails a conscious and deliberate denial of things (material possessions, relationships, abstract ideas, values) that might fragment or render impotent the newly developing self and bond with Self.

• An ability to tolerate ambiguity, change and not-knowing. The individual develops the strength—or skill—of living with fewer guarantees and is able to put up with more insecurity. This is accompanied by growing openness to the true self, to one's own capacity to find solutions, even when these aren't readily available.

• The ability to merge self-and-other interests. By this I mean that the necessary balance between the selfish/selfless choice emerges. Almost all I spoke with called themselves "selfish" people. At the same time each described his or her favorite activities in words that valued service, others, nature, caring, relationships and so on. There was a neat blending of inner/outer realities, a way of gently coming to terms and being receptive to the needs of the environment, or of others, as a high pleasure. Also as the sense of separateness dissolves, this perception of integration grows. The woman who said she needed time to restore herself before having strength to care for others is an example of this selfish/selfless blending. A young carpenter works six months of the year and takes the other six months for leisurely bird-watching and walks in the forest. A sculptor who purposes all his work as giving is yet a third illustration of this harmony between selfish/selfless.

• Creative problem-solving skills grow with each increase in self-awareness and the heightened communication with Self. Individuals are able to really "see" the concrete problem in front of them without inordinate fears or other emotions clouding their mind's problem-solving faculties. They confront the present in fresh terms, not as a repetition of previous moments or out of habitual, mechanistic responses. Improvisation and spontaneous effectiveness seem to grow out of the clarity of what needs to be done in a given situation.

Greater Resourcefulness

No one I spoke to lacked problems to solve. However those in the study solved their problems innovatively. The example of married couples who wanted time alone, yet wanted to stay married, comes to mind. Nowhere in the media or popular wisdom had I come across the idea of consciously designed marital "time-out" (except in the case of dual-career couples who, for the most part, resist the idea of living or working in two separate locations). My interviewees were consistently able to obtain what they needed from others (i.e., from their environment, their work, their friends, etc.) while simultaneously protecting their privacy and while being helpful to others. In other words, there didn't appear to be an exploitive or manipulative edge to their problem-solving styles.

Actualizing individuals develop a worldview analogous to that of the most disciplined, devout monk. They make a radical break with ordinary life as we know it, certainly perceptually—as in the case of my business clients who continue to live and work "as if" they were a part of the mainstream of society but who are emotionally detached to a high degree, probably also in a physical sense. Consider the case of this study's participants: They make a radical perceptual/physical break with convention in order to obey an inner dictate to live truthfully, to live a more conscious, responsible and faithful life. Remaining receptive to the nature and directives of the inner voice takes the same courage, discipline and sincerity as for a religious devotee. In almost all cases, separation from conventional life is costly. In all cases, the detached perception—of course, this is the costliest break—is expensive. Every scrap of reality comes under scrutiny, as these individuals begin to experience their truths and resourcefully correct life to accommodate them, rather than continue living under—and responding to—the seductive perceptual screen of collective beliefs and opinions. People see themselves as they are—not as their egotistical self or idealized image would have them be, and this too is painful when what they are turns out to be so much less than what they would be. In the long run, however, it is out of that lucidity that growth and self-respect emerge. For the short term though, especially in the early stages of social transcendence, there is a steep price to be paid.

The work, if it is to be done at all, must be done alone. And this ultimately is the threat of beginning such a process. The socially transcendent are each en route to becoming a minority of one: an authentic individual in a conforming world. Unlike the religious monk, who receives a ready-made life structure and even a good measure of social approval, the socially transcendent individual can be, and can feel, very much alone, cut off from familiar sources of love and belonging.

Fortunately, there are compensations. Not the least of these is an expanding and increased ability to feel and express love in the truest and most generous sense of the word, as well as an

enriched capacity to experience oneself as part of an interrelated, ✱ ✱✱
whole world.

In other words, the individual—to the extent he or she is actualizing—loses the sense of separateness at the core of all anxiety: the anxiety that signals the unlived, thwarted life. In our next chapter we will explore some of the manifestations of authenticity as it expresses its mature and caring love through work. For it is through work and interpersonal activities that the actualizing best demonstrate their sense of relatedness, responsibility and stewardship.

4

The Developmental Side of the Stewardship Pattern

> Society depends for its existence on the inviolable personal solitude of its members. Society, to merit its name, must be made up not of numbers, or of mechanical units, but of persons. To be a person implies responsibility and freedom, and both these imply a certain interior solitude, a sense of personal integrity, a sense of one's own reality and of one's ability to give himself to society. Thomas Merton[1]

Being socially transcendent does not mean living in isolation. As we have seen, people experience social transcendence regardless of economics, social circumstances or living arrangements. Their detachment becomes activated the moment they are aware of having a distinct self, a self whose reality flows from a sacred ground of being, not the society in which they live.

This clarity ultimately provides them with the distance needed for their ongoing communion with the higher Self—a communion that then stimulates and supports their growth into wholeness. As the individual's whole-seeing and whole-thinking develop—as he or she begins to separate from the self's "little" perceptions, ego-interests and preoccupations—there opens up a truthful relationship with others, a relationship based on a life that itself is becoming more authentic. In fact, it is only through the vitality and trustworthiness of the authentically lived life that we sustain relatedness in a generic sense. Such relatedness requires strength, the ability to overlook the foibles and foolishness of others and the patience and maturity to give to others without becoming emotionally scattered or swept away by the instabilities, pressures or manipulations of the outer world.

As people discover their true identities, they are also more able to give the gift of themselves, because there is a real self to give. In concert, the study participants expressed the desire to give of themselves, a desire grounded in a perspective that sees the other-*as*-self. They also demonstrated an increased ability to act in ways that contribute to the well-being, care and needs of others. I call this tendency the stewardship pattern.

In the original Judeo-Christian tradition, the word *stewardship* meant servanthood: the care and management of God's resources, both material and human. This idea had its beginnings in the earliest chapters of the Old Testament, where man had no existence apart form God; where *Abba, Yahweh* and *God* were all words used to describe the supreme Father to whom all were responsible, apart from whom no one had any life at all, and who had created man to care for the earth. Genesis 2:15 teaches us, "The Lord God took the man and put him in the Garden of Eden to till it and keep it." Not only is man created to take care of the garden, but he is also expected to nurture and protect all life in it.

Judging from the many times in Scripture that God counsels and reprimands man on this issue, humans may not have been disposed to carry out God's high expectations. While equality and justice are special themes throughout both the Old and the New Testaments, it is in the Old Testament that we read of God dealing most harshly with those who forget their obligations to behave responsibly toward others. God takes an active interest in how we treat others and manage our lives and affairs in general, and regularly intervenes to punish those who—like Cain—misbehave or who are callous toward others. God takes keen interest in all who are his. God frees the oppressed and helps them through their trials and sufferings. God's clear and continual message to man in this early stage of his time on earth is that socially responsible behavior is the expected standard.[2] "The earth is the Lord's and the fulness thereof," Psalm 24:1 (KJV) instructs—man is supposed to take an active, responsible caretaker's role if he desires to fulfill God's plan.

Thus, the original premise of stewardship had a threefold root: there is a responsible servant in the form of each and every *human;* there is a definite entrustment to the servant of everything that belongs to God; and there is an ultimate accounting to God for the way the earth and all its people are cared for.

Within this traditional perspective, we glorify God as we make good and prudent use of whatever we have been given to manage. We also honor God's expectations as we serve others and treat them as our brothers and sisters.

Because the Bible can be read and interpreted on many levels, the early concept of stewardship could be understood through a psychological model as well as a religious one. Viewing the stewardship concept developmentally, we might come to understand God—as described in the Old Testament—as a stern, ever watchful parent who knows that his young, immature children need a lot of training in self-control before they can internalize the idea of relating kindly, lovingly, properly to others and to things.

Immature, underdeveloped people are impulsive. The opportunistic are self-involved. In the mature human, greed and self-obsession have given way to generosity, selflessness and a disciplined will that, finding a deep joy in charity, can give to others. When we speak of "arrested development," we mean adults whose grown-up bodies are actually housing children. These are the narcissists who, despite advanced chronological age, see narrowly, fearfully, perhaps in an infantile way. They are emotionally blocked by childish responses or rebellion, fixated at the very point they encountered obstacles, but stopped growing. Some experience that should have been dealt with, overcome and assimilated was repressed, leaving such individuals still reacting to life and trying to solve daily problems out of the framework of the old, infantile perception.

For the immature, fear is often a prime motivator for right action. Rules, laws, restrictions and the threat of punishment for forbidden actions are all ways to insure that the individuals control themselves. A childish mentality does not love self-restraint, so it requires external rules for its and others' safety and well-being. For example, a youngster needs strict guidelines and forceful "logical" consequences to learn to leave matches alone or to remember to look both ways before crossing the street. In like fashion, humankind in its childhood needed authoritarian guidance, even occasional slaps on the hand, to learn to behave. That's not how *love* develops.

It is only later in the story of our human evolvement that a novel element—spiritual love—gets introduced. We first read of that love, *agape,* in the New Testament through the radical teachings of Jesus Christ, a perspective and call that continues to impact the stewardship principle today. No doubt that quality emerged only when humankind was ready—even if only to a slight degree—to hear what Jesus taught. His actions, expectations and life demonstrate what it means to love from a generous, mature spirit. Jesus shows us how to express mature love. He reflects—through every word and deed—how to forgive and minister to others, how to care for them and how to make choices from our highest, most responsible self.

These are not easy lessons to learn; the earliest Christians also apparently needed lots of repetition. The Pauline epistles contain frequent lectures in which Paul and other disciples try to get their followers to grow up. "But I, brethren, could not address you as spiritual men, but as men of the flesh, as babes in Christ. I fed you with milk, not solid food; for you were not ready for it; and even yet you are not ready, for you are still of the flesh. For while there is jealousy and strife among you, are you not

...behaving like ordinary men?" (1 Cor 3:1–4). There are other instances of scolding; for example, Hebrews 5:12–14: "For though by this time you ought to be teachers, you need someone to teach you again the basic elements of the oracles of God. You need milk, not solid food; for every one who lives on milk is unskilled in the word of righteousness, for he is a child. But solid food is for the mature...."

Many are rightly concerned that the deeper aspects of faith, of God, of man's intimate relationship to God cannot be absorbed or properly handled by those who are still childish in understanding and response.

From a developmental frame of reference, it is clear Jesus of Nazareth was a whole, self-realized, completed "personality"—the epitome of the illumined man. His active, eternal demonstration of love exemplifies what *human* love could be, were we spiritually mature ourselves. Love, reliability, empathic understanding, a generous spirit, the ability to experience another as oneself, keeping our word, an ability to affirm life fully in the face of death—these are all traits that flow from a supremely well-defined, elevated consciousness, from a will that gives us the faith and self-mastery to say, "Thy will be done," and from the commitment that supplies the wherewithal to follow through with a task or promise, regardless of sacrifices or discomfort. While Cain asks "Am I my brother's keeper?" the New Man responds by selflessly giving his life for his brothers.

Christ's teachings on brotherly love in the New Testament call us to the highest levels of functioning, to the highest faculties of consciousness. When he tells us to love God above all, our neighbors as ourselves, it is because, at his ground of being, Jesus is love—is knowing that transcends self-concern or fear of punishment. That love is a by-product of spiritual development, our willing self-discipline, and the grace of our newly found way and anointing power born of intimate relationship with God. Thus,

Jesus advocated boldly choosing to act from a deep trust, of union with the Father and a sense of interrelationship with others.

His life and teachings, and those of his disciples, remain a radical call for self and social transformation—"radical" because not automatic; radical because these teachings run counter to our all-too-natural tendency to be self-serving; we're asked to forget our own interest, family or community. The transcendent or spiritual perspective refines those high faculties that would enable us to be potential instruments of the Good. In other words, Jesus asks us to become fully human—in the sense of cultivating a broad, compassionate humanity—to serve from love instead of from fear or a sense of obligation, to demonstrate the divine love that asks for everything we have. It is in this kind of maturity, in this spiritual growth we find true stewardship rooted.

Contemporary American society offers many examples of stewardship in action through its social and environmental programs. These, despite political setbacks, appear to be growing. The environmentalist movement stresses the needs of the future as it seeks to protect, respect and preserve wildlife, the wilderness, alternative fuel sources and our earth's resources. The increasing network of local, national and international agencies, both secular and religiously based, that have sprung up to house, feed and protect the rights of the poor and the homeless is another stewardly movement. The massive national attention and community support now given to battered women and children, the elderly and the handicapped are yet further examples of citizens collectively demonstrating their care for and feelings of relatedness to others. These programs, however political they may appear and however slick their marketing campaigns sound, are, at the individual level of giving, signs that the *idea* of stewardship—the idea of caring for others and a world entrusted to us—exists in the nation's collective consciousness.

Individual stewardship is expressed as a potent giving of self. It is egoless in that, through giving, the mature individual serves higher needs than his or her own comfort, safety and gratification. We give when we directly experience other's needs and concerns as our own; good stewards give not because of external pressures, fear of retribution or a desire to impress others. Good stewards give because their hearts are made more joyful, their lives more meaningful by their giving.

Of course, individuals contribute in differing ways and degrees, both of their material possessions and of themselves. But for the spiritually mature, gifts of self always flow out of a full heart, unselfishness and love, *agape*—concern for the other. As we will see in the next chapter, that spirit of giving transforms duty into pleasure and livelihood into calling.

5
Gifts of Self As Stewardship

Like good stewards of the manifold grace of God,
serve one another with whatever gift each of you has
received.   1 Peter 4:10

Gifts of the self are so varied that there is no easy way to cat-
egorize them. These include giving time to others or getting
involved with their problems —even the projected concerns of
future generations, such as the stewardly acts of environmental-
ists or volunteers. A gift of self might be our application of energy
and effort to a vocation in ways that allow natural aptitudes to be
shared. One's gift *might* be the development of patience. Or learning to live harmoniously with others, with nature or with the
demands of an occupation or organization. There are gifts of
time, money or one's own character, say, providing strengths from
our deepest psyche or becoming a source of inspiration or sup-   ✳
port to others.

Whatever its form, the potency and force of love is always
present to some degree in true contribution. We have seen that
mature spirited love is dependent on the relative presence of
virtue, empathy and an evolved self that has something of sub-
stance to give.

In offering some gift of self, we give from strength—*not* from
a weakened, fearful or exploitive self; not from submission to external pressures or to manipulate another through our giving.

Because each of us is distinctive, as we refine our specific
talents and skills, we will have much to offer from the wellspring
of the core self. To speak of giving from any other perspective is
to relegate the act to a mechanistic, even negative, response.

The attitudes and actions of those in this study reveal a threefold psychology of stewardship. The first aspect of this pattern is fruitfulness: we as givers desiring a deeper, fuller use of our own gifts. We want to discover our unique talents and use these so as to offer something of value to others. In other words, productivity is tied to genuine giving, which, in turn, is linked to self-knowledge. "Know thyself" would, in this context, mean "give what is rare and fine of yourself."

The second characteristic of stewardship is that the giver experiences a kinship with others. This quality of relatedness is significant because, as noted, it is impossible to genuinely care for others, to be considerate of the earth and all its life forms, without heartfelt empathy. All living creatures, including ourselves, are part of the Garden, as it were.

Paradoxically, the socially transcendent who, at first, may step outside the bounds of conventional life are uniquely qualified to be good stewards. These individuals ultimately overcome their feelings of fear, separation and alienation—all symptoms of learned powerlessness and an underdeveloped spiritual awareness. As actualizing, whole individuals they then achieve a sense of union with others that amplifies the giving impulse.

Third, good stewards develop a progressively potent, dynamic love. The individuals in my study exhibited that love through thoughts, works and interpersonal activities.

This chapter examines each of these stewardship patterns in more detail and provides an illustration of how these traits were expressed by the study participants.

The first stewardship pattern is a desire to discover, then express, one's own unique gifts and use these to benefit self-and-other. Study participants viewed work as an integral part of life, not as something split into a duel sphere of work versus personal life. Work is an activity that emanates from the innermost self, as a mirror of self. Whether these people worked in solitude—as writers, researchers or artists—or as educators or in business, they viewed their work as a natural, spontaneous and seemingly effortless extension of themselves. In this way, they translated individual gifts into "fruits" others could enjoy.

The magical artist Ben Shahn once said that every artist who expresses the depth and subjective truths of his life gives something of rare value and wonder to others. In the same way, as socially transcendent individuals develop a better understanding of their unique interior gifts, as they are able to express that self in the outer forms of family, creativity or work, they give something original and truthful to others. Consequently, these gifts retain a vitality, force and freshness that distinguishes them from mundane outcomes usually experienced from daily effort.

For most people, work is only a means to an end—money, security, power, recognition, status. Work is not loved for itself, not seen as an expression or unfoldment of self. However, almost all study participants differed in that they described their work as contributive but easy, like play. Not that they viewed their work as frivolous. Or that they came to it with an irresponsible attitude. Or that it didn't require effort. Work was something they *preferred* to do, almost above all else. They didn't need or desire recreational activities in order to "feel good," to relax or escape job pressures. There was no evidence that participants were using work to stave off feelings of anxiety or to distance themselves from others. There was no comment about outdoing another through work or using it to gain status. Even material gain took a backseat to these individuals' interest and engagement with the tasks and ideals of their work.

For example, a teacher said she felt her work affected eternity. She worked for the "joy of seeing kids learn. I teach in the trust that there is a future for humanity. My work is play. It is self-expression. It gives meaning, structure and purpose to my whole life."

A city manager described his work as "helping me fulfill my destiny. Whether I'm helping the local public school design a curriculum for environmental education or participating in a civic organization or out in the field supervising one of the clean up projects, it makes no difference to me. It's all a way to do what I do best within the context of what others may call 'work.'"

A potter described his work as a "way of seeing." For him, work was a teacher and a mirror. "My working process often dictates to me what to do next [in life]. I have little need for material possessions: the only things I have left are my tools and my car. The answer to all my problems is just to make another pot."

A poet said, "All my time is leisure time, even when I do what is termed 'work.' This is because my work is play. All play/work is important to me, and I take it seriously. Every word is me expressing myself. That can be frightening when I'm off-center and fine when I'm on-center. Anyway I look at it, it's always me in the work."

A carpenter described his working life as less important in terms of what he did than *how* he did it. "I'm very concerned about how I do a job or project, more so than what I do," he said. "The how gives me satisfaction or the impetus to improve myself, and tells me about myself each step of the way. But I don't really feel I have a job or work that's different from the way I am in every part of my life. I am what I do, if you know what I mean— it's basically the same."

These comments help us understand the cohesive self/world/other view that develops in actualizing individuals. From a motivational perspective, such persons are "metamotivated," to use Abraham Maslow's phrase: they are no longer concerned about filling basic needs, such as security, survival or status. Their actions are stirred from within, from the innermost spontaneous core of themselves to express that which they directly experience as real, beautiful and true.

In describing the actualized individual's attitude toward work, Maslow writes:

> ...in all cases, at least in our culture, they are dedicated people, devoted to some task "outside themselves," some vocation, or duty, or beloved job. Generally the devotion and dedication is so marked that one can fairly use the old words vocation, calling or mission to describe their passionate, selfless and profound feeling for their "work." We could even use the words destiny or fate. I have sometimes gone so far as to speak of oblation in the religious sense, in the sense of offering oneself or dedicating oneself upon some altar for some particular task, some cause outside oneself and bigger than oneself, something not merely selfish, something impersonal.[1]

Such attitudes toward work naturally lead us to the second pattern of stewardship: the feeling of relatedness. Some study participants, sounding much like citizens of the Old Testament, said that they felt a "duty" toward others. As one woman put it, "I'd say we have an obligation to help the poor, the hungry, those in prison. In short, we have a duty to take care of others."

Most were more joyful about the whole matter of giving, expressing their sense of oneness with others as a richly felt fusion with all of life, a unity experienced as sacred.

As later chapters reveal, these feelings are probable signs that we possess at least a bit of the mystic sense, experiencing ourselves as part of an intricate, infinite web of creation.

Said one study subject, "I feel we're all divine, all linked mysteriously, while each of us remains separate, unique, even mundane. This separate/unique and related/linked paradox means we need to respect, even encourage, the diversity amongst ourselves, maintaining a clear core of self, all while serving each

cultural identity
thru preservation
of its art

other." Someone else wrote, "I feel myself to be pretty much like others in that our basic needs are the same. Bottom line, we all want the same things: a place in the sun, respect, the ability to take care of ourselves and our own, and the hope that we'll live forever, surrounded by those we love and need."

People perceive their relatedness to others and to the world only as they internalize the ethical, integrated characteristics of spiritual maturity and illumination. Of course, there are degrees of such maturity and illumination. As we live our relatedness through various aspects of life, we come to view ourselves as integrated, in reciprocity with others. Lacking this perception, wholeness cannot emerge; others will always appear to have characteristics we disown.

Eventually the feeling that others are much like us eliminates the sense of separation and isolation. That development allows us to bond to others, as well as to the deep part of the self. The growing sense that one is part of everyone can be expressed in many ways: as a poignant caring for other, as feelings that another's joy and pain is much like one's own, as self-acceptance, as nonjudgment. By accepting our potential for shortcomings we more humbly take our place among other human beings.

Whatever words they used to describe that sense of relatedness, all study participants reflected some degree of connectedness. This is evident both from what they *say* they feel and what they do to serve others in their communities.

One woman said, "I seem to care intensely about those who are victims of injustice. Sometimes now I feel a growing unity, a responsibility and an obligation to people in general." Another, a retired woman, talked about her community stewardship in this way: "My work is now gardening, canning, 'baby' sitting, tutoring, playing the piano in a nearby nursing home, visiting prisoners and looking for other ways to 'work' with and serve others. I hope to get better, be better as a person, as I get older—I'll be sixty-three next month. I believe in mutual support. My husband and I cooperate with neighbors to a significant degree. We're even living in a fledgling community where cooperation, in terms of growing food collectively and exchanging needed services, is the expected standard. And a satisfying thing it is at that."

A retired woman noted her sense of relatedness governed her life choices and activities. Although she had worked as an accountant throughout her professional life, she originally wanted to enter some sort of Christian service. For various reasons, that goal didn't materialize, so she used her business and accounting skills to earn a livelihood, devoting herself to community service projects and church work in her off-work hours. She said:

> I've known since I was eighteen that I wanted to do some kind of service work. I was fortunate in that I worked at an easy job and had energy and time after hours to work with people. I've looked for ways to serve others, to fill a need that might exist. I feel much happier when I'm doing that. Now that I'm retired, I can give all my time to service and church-related projects. I teach creative writing to an adult group, I teach reading to another group through the Literary Volunteers of America, and I've always been active—even at the national level—in my church.
>
> I recall back when I was a youngster, in church they'd pass around collection barrels to gather tithes and offerings. The slogan on those barrels was, "Others first." That slogan has stuck with me all these years.
>
> I'm seventy-three now, and have learned that when I put my mind on others, it helps me get my mind off myself, not in a way that puts me down, but in a way that lets me forget myself, even helps me feel happier. I don't give of myself because I "should"—I don't like the word "should" because that makes me feel I have

to do something, and takes the joy out of it for me. I'm just selfishly doing what makes me happy.

Other study participants described how they acted on their feelings of connectedness through their work. A teacher put it this way:

> If you've read *Goodbye Mr. Chips* then you know how I feel about my work. For me teaching is a way of developing a family—not in the personalized way most people think of, but as Mr. Chips described it, in the final pages of the book: When someone told Chips that it was sad he didn't have children of his own, he answered, "It's wrong to think I've had no children. I've had hundreds and hundreds of children." And that's exactly how I feel. I believe I'm doing a service for lots and lots of people. The things I do, whether it be teaching or involving myself in my church, have a sort of social mysticism for me. It's how I engage in the world, and at the same time experience God in myself and in others. These things I do are truly how I bring God into being.

An environmentalist said feelings of connectedness affected his approach to work:

> I have a reverence for nature, a humility regarding past generations, a desire to honor some of the traditions of the past and those who have come before me. Being raised in a Sunday school, Christian environment must have influenced me as I was growing up. I recall a sense of outrage when I heard of social injustices and saw them happening to people. I guess I could call my desire to be concerned, my need to translate this con-

cern into practical outcomes, a "calling." If I were to describe the personal attributes that have helped me be happy and productive, I'd say caring for others lets me be happy. This feeling is grounded in an optimism and what I can only call a gentleness for all life. Caring for others and the environment fills me with happiness.

Another man, a carpenter and naturalist, described his perceptions of his life and work in this way:

Loving is meaning. It's probably through my work that I express love. These days I experience a lot of love just being part of this lovely forest. For example, there's a bird here called a nighthawk. It comes by every year around this time, is very endearing, and has become a regular visitor here. If I had to identify what it would mean to be my highest self, I'd say it would be learning to live as softly as possible, without making a big footprint on the earth.

The common thread through these statements seems the sense of unity each one feels with others and the world. These individuals speak from a worldview that sees no separation, no real strangers. This is not to say that they feel the same emotions as everyone they meet, or believe they must conform to the wishes and standards of others, or relate completely to the values of others. Rather, to the extent that they are most truly themselves, they experience a link to others, a bond to the natural world. The unitive sense means oneness—not sameness. It is the foundational attitude for a stewardly giving of self.

Finally, the third quality of stewardship—the giving of self through a strong emotion of love—flows spontaneously out of that interrelated worldview. As we have seen, some study participants expressed their giving as "duty," and hadn't yet reached that openhearted level of development where they actively *desired* to give; their stewardship seemed to be more an intellectual "head" matter rather than a heart concern.

For those in the study who are more highly actualized, serving others becomes an essential part of life, almost something about which the individual has no choice. To them, work and leisure are integrated activities. Thus, all life is perceived as service. The total psyche is dedicated to giving, even for those working in isolation, such as writers, artists and scientists. *Not* to give would be experienced as deprivation, as if something were missing in life.

Those who spoke of work in strongly vocational, devotional terms exemplify the highly actualized individual's way of giving through inborn talents. These people *become* their work; they sacrifice everything to it, not in a strained, pressure-ridden or unbalanced way, but rather in a manner that creates a fully functioning, effective result. One is totally absorbed by the work. The potency of such a working life becomes obvious. These sorts teach us about the power and dynamism of love, since that marks their giving.

In his classic book *The Art of Loving,* Erich Fromm reminds us that love involves more than receiving, that love is a fruitfulness that strengthens us as individuals rather than diminishing us:

> Love is an activity, not a passive affect; it is a "standing in," not a falling for…the active character of love can be described by stating that love is primarily giving, not receiving…[and] for the productive character, giving is the highest expression of potency. In the very act of giving I experience my strength, my wealth, my power….Giving is more joyous than receiving because in the act of giving lies the expression of my aliveness.[2]

The statement of a young environmentalist in the study serves as an excellent illustration of just this kind of aliveness. Living on less than five thousand dollars per year, he describes his life this way:

> I'd say the quality of my life is rich. That's the way I feel when I wake up in the morning. My house is small, and I live without electricity, without many of the amenities people call "modern." But when I look around me, I see that everything is luscious: I live in a beautiful house, I'm surrounded by forests, sunlight and gorgeous, opulent trees. Culturally, I'm surrounded by people who care for me, and whom I care about. Politically and religiously, there's every type of activity I could wish for. I get lots of hugs, affection, approval and kindnesses of all types from people in my community. I feel rich. There's no other way to describe it.

Although he isn't specifically talking about work, his vibrancy and perceptual sense of abundance and beauty stems, at least in part, from his total involvement with his work. It has special meaning for him; he describes it as a "calling."

His sentiments do not much differ from those of, say, John Muir or Thomas Merton as he reflects upon the richness of his own life. Even though Merton lived in a way others might call poor, he would write, "I cannot say I am making much money. I get $45 per month, plus room and board. Yet, the life I lead here is as happy as the richest kind of life and, as far as I am concerned, just as comfortable. How can I write about poverty when, though I am in a way poor, yet I still live as though in a country club?"[3]

The consciousness of abundance is a characteristic of actualizing individuals. They experience love as their ground of being, attaining a deep awareness of the infinite richness, intricacy and order of the universe (as we will see in a later chapter on the peak experience)—an awareness that itself is a sign of the illumined mind. To a great extent, that consciousness is "goal-less," feels as if it *has* everything, and is motivated to give from the experience of having attained everything needed. Because actualized individuals experience themselves as "completed" (i.e., needing nothing, not having deficits, etc.), they *see* the world richly, *even when* their five senses contradict such subjective opulence.

Later in our interview, the aforementioned environmentalist said that what makes him happy is to give of himself:

> I'm highly involved in this community through my work, and in fact sometimes I get spread too thin and then have to cut back. I will say I experience every activity as fulfilling: I write, I have a radio program which is basically my way of educating large numbers of people. I'm involved in political action in such a manner that I feel I'm accomplishing something of real value. I'm living out the things that mean a great deal to me in my community, and in very practical ways at that. I feel so fortunate to be in a position to give of myself in these ways. The fact that others are willing to receive what I'm giving is a thrill.

A painter described his work in much the same way. His sentiments let us feel the vigor, potency and total commitment that he puts into his art. His subjective state is opulent.

> My work requires commitment of a sort I find hard to express. I never thought of it until now, but I live for the work. This must be what it's like to be a politician; you do it twenty-four hours a day. It's more than work. It's preoccupation with the ideas of your occupation. I live for the work, and I *am* the work. My work seems to be my life. I don't really *go* to work, since I live what I do.

A peace activist helps us understand the similarities between these working attitudes and a religious vocation, even though earlier in our conversation she rejected any notion of having religious feelings herself. "I'm not spiritual," she said of herself. "I'm earthy, perhaps soulful, but I hate all that empty form-without-content which I saw in organized religions and felt when my family and I went to church...so I wouldn't say I am religious or even spiritual now." Nevertheless, later in our interview she described her work in this stewardly way:

> I live my life with a full consciousness of others, including nature, rather than coming from a "me first" point of view. Of course, this attitude is part of everything I do: my work, the way I live, the way I relate to people. I'd say my work is a calling. I can't *not* do it. The most important thing I feel I can do right now is educate people to the dangers of nuclear war. This sense, or calling, has grown steadily over the past two and a half years. I feel everything else I do is secondary to this goal. It's as if I've had a conversion experience and have been taken over by these feelings; in a real way I've been taken over by my desire to share these ideas and convictions with others.

The entire motivational thrust of the stewardship pattern, as seen here, is generous. It originates from the positive, pleasureful and highly charged impulses of the core, actualizing self.

Such individuals go about contributing in what might appear selfish ways. They exclude many conventional activities, perhaps exclude even certain people, from their lives. They have discovered what, for them, has meaning and truth and have taken steps to bring that to fruition in their daily actions. In varying degrees, these people reveal the paradox of wholeness: as they dedicate themselves sacrificially to a self-affirming life (and this is what others will often label as "selfish"), more power and a more abundant ability to love are born.

That "standing-in" sort of love empowers such individuals to be life-affirming—in a broad sense—and also fuels their intuitive leaps of faith. Ultimately, these leaps spark further strength and will to give selflessly to others. The pacifist in our study describes how concentration, discipline and purposefulness increase as wholeness is cultivated:

> I don't indulge myself as I used to. I now control my social life so as not to get involved in things that distracted me from my work, but which are not very interesting or purposeful for me. I'm so focused now, much more than most people I know....What I want to do more than anything else—more than I thought I could want anything—is to educate people to the dangers of nuclear war, and in that way help build a safe and peaceful place for all of us to live.

The actualizing develop along the lines of their innate strengths. For the mystic—an elevated and distinct spirituality—these strengths are decidedly transpersonal, transcendent and religious, as is the development.

Our next chapter describes the way in which the mystic interprets all of life, including work, as having its source in God. The mystic lives, works and relates to others within the context of a unitive or God-consciousness. Meister Eckhart, a great if not the greatest mystic, exemplifies the unitive consciousness with these words: "The wood does not change the fire into itself, but the fire changes the wood into itself. So are we changed into God, that we shall know him as he is."[4]

And so it is that our next chapters describe how the mystic becomes more and more filled with the awareness of God.

PART TWO
The Way of the Mystic

Cheap grace is the grace we bestow on ourselves.... Costly grace is the treasure hidden in the field; for the sake of it a man will gladly go and sell all that he has. It is the pearl of great price to buy which the merchant will sell all his goods.

Costly grace is the gospel which must be sought again and again, the gift which must be asked for, the door at which a man must knock. Such grace is costly because it calls us to follow.... It is costly because it costs a man his life, and it is grace because it gives a man the only true life.

Dietrich Bonhoeffer, The Cost of Discipleship

6
The Mystic Type along the Way

What human beings through all centuries and throughout the world are really good at is defending themselves against the love of God.

Study participant, Alabama

Only in mystics do we observe the full expanse of humankind's *spiritual* potential. For the mystic, daily life and moment-to-moment thought—the large and little events—are linked intimately with spiritual encounter. The mystic taps into and cultivates the deepest levels of the intuitive and subjective self so much so that writers such as Evelyn Underhill and Richard Bucke, long-time researchers of the mystic type, suggested that mystics develop new and extended faculties of perception. These lift them "above" other people, perhaps even marking a species shift within our human family. What sets the mystics apart is that they are "in love with the Absolute," to use Underhill's phrase.

Mystics are a definite type. They have a distinctive life's course. Their mission, regardless of country or culture of origin, is always the same: to find their way "back" to God or that Absolute Reality which they sense is the One True Reality, and from which they sense they've come.

A key difference between mystics and all others is that their spiritual eyes have been opened, and they have "seen." From the chaos of life's early inner confusion, mystics awaken to an illumined mode of being. They are in a state of *being*, rather than, like most people, seeking to become. Mystics are our poets and artists; our intuitional, creative thinkers; our inventors and, of course, our saints.

They experience such a high degree of interior richness that with little effort, or so it may seem to others, they develop their latent powers of transcending ordinary, consensus reality.

One study participant described how he transcends normal reality:

> Last Sunday, [in church] I tried a new way of centering down, and was prompted to try Eckhart's way.... Graphically, this could be called putting oneself in God's shoes and "knowing" from this perspective. As I felt my way into this there was speaking within me, like within the Old Testament prophets, the voice of God, using human words....What was remarkable about this was the heightened sense of needs which I perceived. I "knew" everyone, including myself, very much more clearly and intuitively than before. I "knew" with a sort of detachment which let me focus on the needs of others without getting messed up with my own emotional responses. This clear-seeing, which I'd rather not call clairvoyance, seemed to go beyond my previous perceptions of people. I have since rather easily been able to return to this without being forced, stilted or artificial. Romans 8:26 may point to this mode of prayer; otherwise, I have never encountered it in reading before.

Because mystics are transmuting the ordinary self into the higher Self, the way or journey of the mystic is fully integrated with their psychology. The mystic's psyche and his or her lifestyle are merged.

The mystic's experience gave birth to the whole sphere of transpersonal psychology. That has been described as different from ordinary therapies (e.g., Freudian, Adlerian, etc.) in one critical way: while conventional therapies help people cope with their fears, anger, trauma and passions, transpersonal psychology helps them awaken spiritually. If the mystic's ability to see and hear things of a transcendent reality can be trusted (and I believe it can), we might say that the mystic represents the individual who is illuminated, or at the very least is in the process of being so.

Very few of those in this study consider themselves true mystics. However, my hunch is that some of the study participants are approaching a state of illumination, or *being*. I have therefore included, throughout the rest of this chapter, comments by only those few participants who readily identify with the mystic's profile (who, for example, recall their transcendent experiences, are able and willing to describe their spiritual or mystical experiences, etc.). I hope to underscore the principles of the spiritual psychology of mysticism by illustrating these features with the words and sentiments of those who articulated and wholeheartedly embrace the mystic stance.

Underhill cites three elements that characterize the mystic way. I am indebted to her research in that it serves as a foundation for my own. She states:

1. Mysticism is a transformative approach to life, rather than a theoretical "playing" with ideas.

2. Mysticism involves spiritual activity, representing the individual's absorption and deepening relationship with God. This activity absolutely influences and dominates the mystic's path and is inseparable from it. Thus mystic and "path" are one.

3. The mystic's dominant life-emotion becomes love. This subjective stance and worldview shows itself in a progressively strengthened dedication of will toward the things of God: the expression of spiritual intent in daily life; service to God through work, relationships and everyday choices; and sacrifices of the physical/mental body all experience and glorify the Divine.

Although mystics may not "appear" to be active participants in the world (i.e., they may be more contemplative and thus seem

the Divine

passive, "nondoing" in the Taoistic sense, than others), in fact their entire worldview is dedicated to God. As Thomas Merton often wrote, their life's work is *being*; is life itself; is not specifically one profession or another.

First, the practical, transformative nature of the mystic's life might be compared to a progression of rebirth. That usually starts with a conversion experience that we will examine in our next chapter. Suffice it to say now that the mystic process culminates not in a life-terminating way, but with the individual's complete experiential union with God (as opposed to merely intellectualizing about that). That rebirth can take a lifetime to manifest. Or it can happen in an instant, as apparently occurred with Saint Paul. In typical mystic's phraseology Paul said, "To live is Christ, and to die is gain." His words are permeated with that rhapsodic ardor that characterizes the mystic's rebirth. Once the seed of rebirth takes hold, these individuals are never again their own. By a complete renewal of mind and heart they live life in the Absolute, their entire being consumed by the Transcendent consciousness.

Mystics long to know Ultimate Reality as their own by direct experience, by intimate relationship to God. One individual in the study, for example, a carpenter living in solitude in California's coastal redwoods, described his longing for God this way: "The one constant in my life, the one integrative desire, is my longing to connect with the unity of the universe. I guess you'd call that God. This is the one thing of value in my life, the thing that keeps me going."

Another man, also living in solitude, wrote me a follow-up letter, after our in-person interview, describing his "thirst for transformation": "I consider my involvement in [this project] one of the active concerns in my life because it directly mirrors the transformation I have been going through, am going through …and desire to 'complete.'"

Another participant said, "I see an importance in the moment, *this* moment, this present point when everything is ending and all is beginning. I try to touch this as often as possible."

Underhill outlined two distinct thrusts to full mystic consciousness. One is the increasing vision or consciousness of God; the other is the inner transmutation of self, the rebuilding or restructuring of self on an inward, deep, all-pervasive level. Neither pattern can be accomplished, as we shall see, without the complete transcendence of narcissism. Eckhart seemed to call this "emptiness," where one no longer clings to outer things, not even oneself. Underhill writes: "The end and object of this 'inward alchemy' will be the raising of the whole self to the condition in which conscious and permanent union with the Absolute takes place; and man, ascending to the summit of his [existence], enters into that greater life for which he was made."[1]

True mystics are not merely involved with esoteric thoughts or beautiful images of God and heaven. They are totally absorbed in a life-movement, a journey in which the psyche or essential self comes to life with, and *in,* God. This "coming to God," *is* the journey. Its goal is to live in such a way that there is no distinction between daily activity (i.e., one's business, chores like washing dishes or scrubbing floors, walking in the streets, shopping, etc.) and prayer, worship or remembrance of God. In other words, the true mystic desires that life be subsumed in, and with, the presence of God.

Stages along the mystic way have been interpreted differently by various writers, but fall into several distinct levels of growth. The intuitional step is first, best described as an inner prompting, perhaps a sudden insight, when we sense there is more to life than ordinary living currently reveals. This awakening can come either as a core religious experience (also called a conversion experience: a moment of illumination, or a peak experience during which the mind grows still and thought "vanishes") or as an ongoing, increasing "knowing" that Absolute reality is the one (and *only*) true and worthwhile life.

However it starts, the mystic's journey involves a subsequent pulling away from the world: a distancing, subjective detachment or impersonal sense that is contemplative and simplified and may parallel what in mystic terminology is called "purification." That life-posture unites the individual most completely with the transcendent nature of reality by lessening the pulls and enticements of the world[2] and, ultimately, enhancing fusion with God.

These stages follow the configuration of social transcendence described earlier. We have seen that an individual's wholesome social detachment eventually leads to growth. The mystic's path also involves initial detachment, and like the secular monk, the mystic reassesses old ideas, images, cultural beliefs and past programming. Each must also assimilate and integrate new perceptions, values and sensibilities into daily life.

However, whereas the "monk"—like, say, Dorothy Day, the Catholic social activist—seeks answers in social solutions, mystics *always* organize their life through spiritual solutions. They find answers in the Transcendent. When mystics do act in the social sphere, their motivating drive is always to pay homage to the Truth, to God. Their poetry or prayers or books reflect that silent, "small still voice" within. After all, the term *self-transcendence* means that the former persona or "mask" is dissolving; that the lesser, culturally defined self with its idealized images and constricting, socially produced outer shell collapses, giving way to the larger, real Self.

I would guess, and only further research could confirm, that the mystic's journey is a natural extension of inner work that already has begun in the socially transcendent individual. But the inner transformation that takes place in the mystic extends beyond that of the secular monk in that mystics seek to live as prayer, in complete and intimate relationship with God. Secular monks—however detached and stewardly they may be in their efforts—do not always express themselves in spiritual terms. Mystics always do. "The mystic," wrote Underhill, "...dwells in a world unknown to other men. He pierces the veil of imperfection, and beholds Creation with the Creator's eye."[3]

A study participant articulated her own "awakened spirit" this way:

> I feel as though I'm walking with God all the time now. Little, insignificant things happen to me that make me feel his presence. I feel he's a part of me and that I'm a part of him. There is a sort of inner light in and around me, although I know it's not a visible thing, and I don't actually visualize it. The point of all of this is that I've gained the strength to live a more potent life, a genuine and authentic life, a life of kindness. Some of my friends wanted me to go with them on a trip to the Holy Land, with our church—you know, to be nearer to God. But I told them, "No." I don't have to walk in the Holy Land or travel to some other part of the world to know God. He's with me all the time and everywhere.

The mystic's life-altering path always results in a radical dropping away of the former self and a restructuring of self in the discernment of God. Gradually or suddenly, the mystic relates differently to others, abandons social and material interests in favor of another realm, the Transcendent. This life-movement makes physical, social and personal sacrifices possible, even mandatory. These would be experienced by anyone, but for the mystic it is major psychic surgery; such is the currency, urgency and intensity of the called-for sacrifices. Alterations might range from seemingly minor ego-bruising choices to the complete surrender of key comforts, securities or even life itself. Consider the contemporary example of Gandhi, who time and again put himself into harm's way in order to express Truth. Or Julian of Norwich, a Christian contemplative who lived and wrote in a tiny cell over the course of her adult life.

Mystics define their sacrifices as necessary to fulfill a higher Truth. One study participant, describing a difficult choice, put it this way:

> I notice that fear is leaving me, although not entirely. However, I see myself acting more than before in certain risk-taking ways, and doing so with the backdrop of feeling that the death of my body has nothing to do with me. Jesus said that we shouldn't fear the one who would harm our body, and that's becoming clearer to me.
>
> For example, I'm planning to refuse to pay some taxes under the war refusal tax category. There is fear in me, since I live in an area where there's not much support for that kind of thing. This fear, however, is balanced by a certainty, in consciousness, that this is what I must do.... The act represents the way in which I believe the teachings of Christ would have us go.

The costs of the mystic's journey are made even greater by being so private a transition, almost impossible to communicate to others. Again, the transition necessitates self-transcendence: that lifting out, up and away from the socialized, encultured persona as it has been understood by such individuals since infancy. This, too, makes the path costly and explains why it is so difficult to articulate. The mystic chooses to "sell all and follow Me"; is the one who leaves father and mother in order to have his or her life in God.

The mystic path involves many "mini-deaths," to borrow a phrase from one of this study's participants. Gerald Heard, mystic and author, positioned those "mini-deaths" in language familiar to all mystics, while perhaps foreign to others:

> Can we ourselves hope to climb this tremendous way to the Kingdom? Certainly: there will be no Kingdom unless and until we do so climb to that station.... The very first step is to know that I, as I am, am an obstacle to the Kingdom. I must start, before anything else, by cleansing myself out of the way. I must learn, right down to my reflexes, to say and mean and know "Let my name perish, so Thy Kingdom come."[4]

This purifying process, in which we transcend the small self, is often analogized in mystics' writings to the moth drawn to the flame that ultimately kills it: "The lovers who dwell within the sanctuary are moths burnt with the torch of the Beloved's face,"[5] wrote a Persian mystic, aglow with impassioned love for God, who attempted to describe what it is like to draw near to him. The analogy of being burned by the object of adoration is apt: such individuals, while drawn toward that which is highest and best, know intuitively that the small self must "die" to approach their goal.

The way involves a real and difficult crossing, not an imaginary one. The mystic craves an altered way of seeing and hearing. This necessitates, as Heard described, the obliteration of egoistic interests, bodily concerns, self-serving behaviors, narcissism. Study participants who identified with the mystic type expressed their own dying-to-self variously. One woman said that when she was in church, "many things I heard there lifted me out of myself," and brought out a new sense of humility.

Another vivid statement of self-transcendence came from a conversation with, and later a letter from, one of the mystics in the study:

> I believe that life is reached through death. I have experienced minideaths before I could have room for growth. Dying to self and becoming detached from ownership, for example, helped me get closer to others. In general, I saw myself wanting to detach from possessions; this might even have led me to an abandonment of ties. I've also experienced the loss of people close to me—my wife, for instance, who died two years ago—as another death for me. Her death reminded me of my own, not to mention the loss itself. Yet, on the other side of these experiences, I feel strongly affirmed.

In his letter following our conversation, that man expanded his commentary about minideaths at my request:

> At a recent social outing I'd dropped my cool, fallen back to stuttering and even yelled at another person in the heat of an argument…. [After it was over and I was apologizing] I resolved to keep myself on a higher plane and not get trapped again. But how could I tell my fiancée that the bad scene my "old" self made was the ground of birth for a new consciousness? I didn't even try. This restraint was a minideath…a transformation.

His subsequent decision not to explain himself to his fiancée represents his dying to the ego's impulse to set itself in good standing with others, to save face, protect pride. A new consciousness emerges out of that humility or self-denying; a consciousness that, through humility, comes closer to expressing the liberty and power of the higher Self.

This transition from eccentric, self-involvement to life lived ever more consciously through the higher aspects of awareness causes mystics more than any other type to feel as if their entire character structure is coming undone. During this "undoing period" the person often enters a "dark night of the soul," to coin the familiar phrase of Saint John of the Cross. What another might interpret as alienation (from, say, social or family support) or as not fitting in, mystics, in their period of purgation, feel cut off from God; furthermore they cannot get solace from others because others now speak in language that lacks meaning and sounds foolish.

Saint John of the Cross articulated the benefits to be gained from this arid, separative period: namely, because the soul continually remembers God in its yearning for him, it is thus further purified during this lonely phase of life, becoming more capable of being one with him. Such writings console mystics who inwardly sense that no therapy, circle of helpful friends or trusted counselor can bring relief...

> ...from the aridities and voids of this night...the soul draws spiritual humility, which is the contrary virtue to the first capital sin [of] spiritual pride.... For it sees itself so dry and miserable that the idea never occurs to it that it is making better progress than others.... In this condition, souls become submissive and obedient upon the spiritual road.[6]

This passage, and its language, illustrate both the way and the mystic's temperament and further demonstrate the concrete, transformative nature of this *life*-movement. The typical imagery of a mystic's vocabulary involves words of progress, action or ascent toward or away from God: finding, searching, keeping on the way; being "stuck," lost, separated; then illumination: union, arrival, completion. These sorts of terms tell how through the ages mystics have experienced and verbalized their subjective sense of their own position along self-chosen spiritual paths.

"I'm not there yet," was the phrase I heard repeatedly from the mystics in this study. Their statement acknowledges a "location," some higher level of consciousness to which they aspire, as well as their appraisal of their current place along the apprehended path.

A study participant had second thoughts as to whether or not she "belonged" in the study, feeling that she was so far away from the level of consciousness my survey questions were examining. Many weeks after our conversation she wrote: "...maybe I do not belong in that group of individuals your interesting study is about. I cannot tell myself. But since talking with you, [there's] one theological certainty I feel I can count on. That is Albert Schweitzer's principle, presented [to me] as this: 'I am life that wills to live in the midst of other life that wills to live.'"

In reply I assured her that someone who had given such reflection and time to the purpose of the study, as well as to the "theological certainties" of her life, did belong in our study.

Another participant, describing his own "dark night of the soul," said:

> I feel at odds with myself, cut off from conventional life yet not really connected to the Absolute. The thing that keeps me going is the memory of my previous [mystical] experiences and a desire to become one with that transcendent realm I know is real. I get glimpses of this from time to time, as if I'm seeing a friend in an alien world; these experiences give me a sense of stability, self-worth and connectedness. But there are times when I have none of that, and I just hang on, in trust....

The second pattern of the mystic profile, intense spiritual activity, is also highlighted by special language. The words mystics use contain a unique "invitation;" they utilize words to point to the awe, thanksgiving and worshipful awareness of their highest consciousness.

Buddhists, for instance, talk of Nirvana—their "highest happiness." The Hindus, perhaps the most lyrical mystic poets our world has produced, describe God in whispered, reverential, often boldly supernatural terms. Maher Baba, the Hindu avatar, described the Absolute as "the perennial spring of imperishable sweetness."[7] The Bhagavad-Gita's principal hero, Arjuna, is quoted as saying, "O boundless Form, Thou art the Primeval Deity, the Ancient Being; Thou art the Supreme Refuge of this universe; Thou art the Knower, the one to be known and the Supreme Abode. By Thee alone is this universe pervaded."[8]

Sounding much like these enraptured Easterners, yet coming from a completely different cultural tradition, Saint Thérèse of Lisieux described the mere fleeting *thought* of God in similarly ecstatic language when she said that her "heart was overflowing with love and gratitude."[9]

Jacob Boehme, an uneducated shoemaker who later was called the Teutonic Theosopher, wrote,

> No words can express the great joy and triumph which I experienced [i.e., while illumined with the awareness of God].... While in that state, my spirit immediately saw through everything and recognized God in all things, even in herbs and grasses, and it knew what is God and what is His will. Then very soon my will grew in this light, and received a strong impulse to describe the divine state.[10]

These few examples from Eastern and Western mystical writings only skim the surface of the subjective opulence and gladness that signify the mystic's consciousness as it grows, is infused with the Transcendent. So closely knit are thought and bodily responses that God-consciousness (called, by Christians, Christ-Consciousness; and Cosmic-Consciousness by others) may produce a physical response in the mystic's body.

This is a difficult concept to convey. Our next chapter more specifically examines the link between the mystic sense and physical experiences, or alterations, to the physical state. I interviewed one physician, Dr. Lee Sannella, who has researched the physical manifestations of those undergoing the kundalini awakening, related to Hindu meditation practices. Sannella has traced several patterns of bodily response to the movement of kundalini energy (psychic energy). These are, in Sannella's research, related to intense spiritual transformation, or rebirth:

> Spiritual rebirth has become…a well-defined entity….
> It is not simply an altered state of consciousness, but an ongoing process lasting from several months to many years, during which the person passes in and out of different states of consciousness…. [This] can be described as an evolutionary process taking place in the human nervous system.[11]

I feel it essential to say at this point that the mystic's passionate communion with God—the ability to transcend ordinary reality—results in experiential realization, not just an intellectual idea of the Transcendent. Mystics *feel* differently, see and hear what others do not; they "know" God in a more intimate, direct way than before embarking upon their journey. The mystic's whole being becomes permeated with the sense and spirit of God, a phenomenon unique to those possessing the mystic sense, regardless of cultural background. To many, the mystic borders on psychotic. Were it not for the fact that the great heroes, heroines and saints, the great artists and poets and spiritual leaders of humankind have spoken in mystic terms, it would be easy to discount their experience as insane. Their perceptions negate the world of the senses and logic, for "the wisdom of this world is foolishness with God" (1 Cor 3:19).

If we step further to examine the writings of those who try to describe their actual union with God, their moments of illumination, it becomes readily apparent they are *unable* to recount their experience coherently, so great is their joy, so disorienting their perception. In one of his poems, country parson George Herbert noted all he could say was, "...my joy, my life, my crown," when trying to express his love for God.[12]

Many of the mystics in this study said, when asked about their transcendent experience, that they'd had several. Few could describe them to me. Much like Herbert's poem, *love* was the word they fell back on.

One woman tried to find words:

This is most difficult to explain because I'm not expressing myself in earth terms. At times I feel ecstatic—just imagine if you can, the first time you fell in love. You know something wonderful is happening, something more than usual. You can *feel* it, that love welling up inside, or radiating in and out of you. At other times, it's just a great happiness that pervades my entire being. This is so hard to explain....And, when I'm around others who are in their normal, rather negative state, I'd rather not try. I just want to get off by myself and enjoy the exquisite, subtle state I'm in.

Another repeated her sentiment: "When I'm in that most coherent, loving state, I find it difficult to be with others. In a way it's as if I'm completely one with them; in another, it's as if what they're talking about and involved with is a pseudoreality, not real at all."

Brother Lawrence, the French lay brother of the Carmelites who lived in the 1600s, spoke of the "inexpressible sweetness" he tasted when he communed with God.[13]

Walt Whitman, in what is perhaps the most articulate passage about the ordeal of communicating the ecstatic moment, wrote:

> When I undertake to tell the best, I find I cannot.
> My tongue is ineffectual on its pivots,
> My breath will not be obedient to its organs,
> I become a dumb man.[14]

His words reveal the mystic's intense subjective tone as well as the frustration in not being able to communicate what is highest, best, most sacred and real. This frustration heightens the value of self-transcendence, since the individual becomes less and less able to relate to others vis à vis what has prime meaning. Eventually, there seems to develop a "giving up" or a greater yielding. At any rate, as others lose their status as the object of the mystic's time, attention and interest, the mystic's focus turns progressively on a new Object on which to dwell and experience as Reality for life and Being. My sense is that here is a double-edged factor: the divine love, as we will describe shortly, takes hold of the mystic's consciousness and being. But this is not all feelings; the mystic makes a conscious, rational choice to love, to have faith, to live "as if" he or she were in the Absolute, a choice that colors actions and relations.

That love, those choices, further erase the old belief-system— a sweetly painful process which, as a study participant tried to explain, can be like falling in love. This brings us to the third pattern of the mystic profile: love's dominance in thought, emotions and choices.

Impersonal love, described in all the mystic literature of the world, is at once painful and joyful. It has been written of as a "destructive torch...which opens your heart's book,"[15] or as a burning affection for God. Or, as that Love which "makes all that is heavy light and bears evenly all that is uneven."[16] Or, as that Love which "shows no partiality" (Acts 10:34).

Mystics experience yearning for union with God as a purifying, heated emotion that eradicates the things of old, "making all things new again." Mystic writings repeatedly glow with this intense, transformative ardor for the Absolute. The psalmists, prophets and poets of scriptural and mystical literature spoke of their longing for and love of God. In much the same way so did the small handful of study participants who could rightly be called mystics: "To me," wrote the youngest study participant, age twenty-seven, "everything has meaning [because] life is a spiritual journey. My task or purpose here is to rediscover my spirituality, my relationship to God, to Truth, to the Life force in all. I want to find my way back to my own connectedness and to grow in this Truth."

Another said, "I'd have to say my 'inner program' is to realize more of the unity of life and to share that with others. This drives me totally."

Much like good parents want only to give their child the best they have, even when that means self-denial and getting nothing in return, true mystics ask for nothing from God, wishing only to give. This pure desire sharply contrasts with the goal of cults and persons referred to by Underhill as "magicians," who wish to use their knowledge of supernatural powers to gain material possessions or personal glory. We note many such magicians around today.

Mysticism is not acquisitive. It is a giving up of self. Its object is constant: the conscious giving up of materiality in order to transcend the usual physical/mental limits or excesses and have one's life in the Absolute. It is, in other words, the mystic's goal to *be* in, and with, God—not to have intellectual knowledge or special advantage over others.

This utter sincerity and "purity of heart" (to use Kierkegaard's phrase) and the willingness to abolish and annihilate the "personality" mark the deeply instinctive and generous quality of the mystic temperament. Christian mystic Meister Eckhart exemplified this posture. His writing encourages those who would know God to want nothing from him:

> First let us discuss a poor man as one who wants nothing. There are some...who do not understand this well. They are those who are attached to their own penances and external exercises....God help those who hold divine truth in such low esteem! Such people present an outward picture that gives them the name of saints; but inside they are donkeys, for they cannot distinguish divine truth.... So I say that a man ought to be established, free and empty, not knowing or perceiving that God is acting in him; and so a man may possess poverty.[17]

Such inner emptiness is another attribute of genuine mystics and corresponds to the *agape,* causative love in its most humble, nonstriving form. This emptiness is a goal of each deeply spiritual individual, regardless of cultural heritage. The Zen ideal, for instance, of emptying the mind in order to reach enlightenment seems in the same spirit as Eckhart's teachings. At the moment of enlightenment Dogen-zenji, a Buddhist master, exclaimed, "There is no body and no mind!"[18] He realized in a flash that his whole being included everything in the universe, was one with All. Echoing Eckhart's sentiments, the Zen Master Shrunryu Suzuki wrote:

Because people have no...understanding of Buddha, they think what they do is the most important thing, without knowing who it is that is actually doing it.... Without knowing this, people put emphasis on some activity. When they put emphasis on zazen [meditation], it is not true zazen. It looks as if they were sitting in the same way as Buddha, but there is a big difference in their understanding.[19]

For the mystic, purity of intent flows from compassionate love. Indeed, it is only through love in each aspect of life that mystics reach their goal. They "complete themselves" by giving up all. Such giving up or emptying is only accomplished by individuals who act out of love, who above all else transcend self so as to know the One Reality.

7

Illumination and Darkness along the Mystic's Way

> The person in the peak experience usually feels himself to be at the peak of his powers....He feels more intelligent, more perceptive, wittier, stronger, or more graceful than at other times. He is at concert pitch, at the top of his form. This is not only felt subjectively but can be seen by the observer.[1]
>
> Abraham Maslow

The peak experience is critical to any discussion of the mystic's journey, since through it and because of it these individuals gain an overarching and penetrating view into what they are at their best, when they are simply *being* rather than becoming. They experience directly, and this is such a difficult point to convey to nonpeakers, the transcendent nature of reality. They enter the Absolute, become one with it, if only for a life-altering instant. Many have described that as one in which the human mind "stops," as a time when the paradoxical change/changeless nature of the universe reveals itself.

Because the insights and experiences of the peak or illuminative moment are integrative to the mind/body, we will temporarily leave our study participants and attempt to understand the peak experience. This chapter is divided into three parts for the purpose of clarifying the several dimensions of the peak experience; each part deals with a specific aspect of the core religious moment (as the illuminative moment has also been called; it is *exactly* like those private conversion experiences that serve as the foundation stones, or entry point, to all major religious traditions). The three parts of this chapter are: a general overview of the healing aspects of the peak experience, a brief comment about the reception to the mystic experience or resistance to it in Western culture, and finally some words about the dark side of the mystic's growth pattern.

Overview

Through the peak experience we gain an expanded view of ourselves and our world. We're lifted "above" the world and our limitations in a way that resolves personal splits, contradictions and blocks to full functioning. This "lifting up" of self, this resolution of conflicts, gives rise to the term *transcendence,* which, according to the *New Webster's Dictionary,* means going beyond ordinary limits or surpassing normal human experience. Only actual experience explains self-transcendence, but as the words of one study participant indicate, it "cultures" us, brings out our best qualities—and heals us as well: "[This experience] allows me to trust, to let myself accept guidance, spiritual gifts and counsel. It has let me reduce my own feelings of possessiveness and attachment. I am more relaxed, really unfidgety…to a degree unusual for me. I'll go with this, in trust, and find out where this leads me."

In the transcendent moment we literally "take leave of our senses," entering into a larger dimension of life, like those times when we are completely absorbed in watching a brilliant sunset or responding to a crisis exactly as we must in order to protect ourselves and our loved ones. Perhaps we watch ourselves as the actor while we do superhuman, inordinately competent things to make things right. During peak moments we come "out" of ourselves and connect with something infinite, beyond self.

Here is full, pure awareness: we feel ourselves the cause of our creations *and* simultaneously a part of some expansive, sacred All. Here is the nonduality during which we are most innocent, childlike, spontaneous, vulnerable, unguarded, defenseless and open. We are all these things because our separateness (that which, in a previous chapter, one of the study participants linked to "insanity") has ended. We are bonded to a unitive force that creates feelings of worthiness, compassion, love; of being responsible, capable, fully able to do. And, as this chapter's opening quotes suggest, we also appear that way to others:

> [In the peak experience, the person is] more apt to give the impression that it would be useless to try to stop him. It is as if now he had no doubts about his worth, or about his ability to do whatever he decided to do. To the observer he looks more trustworthy, more reliable, more dependable, a better bet. It is often possible to spot this great moment of becoming responsible—in therapy, in growing up, in education, in marriage.[2]

The transcendent instance bestows the sense that all of creation is wonderful, God-filled, orderly and safe. Fears dissolve as if they had never existed, were a lie, a delusion. This sense of safety (which also includes the loss of the fear of death) provides yet another key to why the peak experience heals so profoundly, since much neuroticism and even physical ills thrive on nameless fears and vague, free-floating anxieties.

During, and usually after, the illuminative moment, we perceive everything as brighter, clearer, richer, more lustrous. This expanded perceptual field is etched ever after in mind and further fuels the mystic's path, even enhances ability to recall and *use* the experience for growth.

In fact, my radical suggestion is that none of us cultivate wholeness until, and unless, we have had a peak experience, call it what you will, thus transcending our limited perspective self and meeting ourselves in and as *being*. It is likely that those who have the "cosmic sense" (either through a sudden, intense conversion or almost constant, gradual and lesser doses of peak experiences) are healthier than the norm.

Whatever our faults, we who "peak" are likely to be more autonomous, integrated, open and fully developed than we who haven't transcended or cannot recall such moments or who actively resist the idea. The phenomenon is so closely tied to primary process creativity that it is hard to discuss such attributes without also exploring the peak experience.

Richard Bucke, a physician, extensively studied and catalogued the attributes of those he felt had "cosmic consciousness." He found that his subjects shared several exemplary traits: they were morally elevated, intellectually illumined and had a sense of their own immortality. They had lost their fear of death as well as their sense of sin. Each had had one or more sudden "awakening" experiences, and their personality had an added charm that made them attractive to others. Bucke's description of their appeal sounds remarkably like Maslow's observation of the attractiveness of peakers. Of Walt Whitman, someone with a supremely well-developed mystic sense, Bucke wrote:

> When I first knew Walt Whitman I used to think that he watched himself, and did not allow his tongue to give expression to feelings of fretfulness, antipathy, complaint and remonstrance....After long observation...I satisfied myself that such absence or unconsciousness was entirely real. His deep, clear and earnest voice [contributed to] the charm of the simplest things he said....He never spoke deprecatingly of any nationality or class of men, or time in the world's history...or against any trades or occupations—not even against any animals, insects, plants or inanimate

things, nor any of the laws of nature, nor any of the results of the laws, such as illness, deformity or death. He never complained or grumbled either at the weather, pain, illness or anything else. He never in conversation...used language that could be considered indelicate....He never spoke in anger...never exhibited fear, and I do not believe he ever felt it.[3]

Some of the people in my study fit (although perhaps to lesser degrees) Bucke's catalogue of traits of the cosmically conscious. They have had, and frequently "enter," the peak experience—as we shall see. Their primary interest is the Absolute, the values of Being-cognition and, like Whitman and others in Bucke's research, they never complained, grumbled or spoke of needing any "thing" to round out their joy and make it full.

Subjects like truth, justice, beauty, the Absolute or Transcendent state are of high interest to them, and they express a desire to live in a way that exemplifies the qualities of that which is highest and best in them. It is as if their consciousness has become imprinted with the qualities experienced during, and gained through, self-transcendence. In varying degrees, they express a loss of fear (e.g., of death, scarcity, "what-will-others-say?" or defying convention). Of this, one participant wrote me a letter asking: "How can we experience the scriptural teaching, 'Perfect love casts out fear'? The full range of human fear has at its center the fear of death. Each time we succumb to a fear we experience a little death, and through each overcoming of a fear we are reborn. More fully, the conquest of fear is analogous to dying in that we risk losing something in the process, yet gain a new life as the result."

The peak experience conditions or prepares us for death because during it, our "ego" (i.e., separate sense, the personal "I") vanishes. With this vanishing goes the fear of death, since the ego-istic small I keeps those fears in place, believing as it does that there is a death, that is to say, a no-life condition to fear. When we join something so much larger, eternal, infinite even with the disappearance of the separate sense of self, our fear of death dissolves.

Some of the study participants remarked that their peak experiences awakened them to a living vitality so much greater than they had known previously.

One woman wrote, "I have had many awareness experiences of transcendence. These have changed my life in that I felt I touched the depth of existence, the incredible. I've retained a sense of awe, as well as the knowledge that 'It' is there, if I can learn to be open enough, trusting enough."

Another in her seventies said, "At age eighteen I had several peak spiritual experiences. These transformed my life and caused me to take positive action toward a definite life's direction. [As a result] my life's philosophy is tied to a real sense of God. Since college my life's verse has been summed up by Deuteronomy 33:27, 'The eternal God is my dwelling place, and underneath are the everlasting arms.'"

Another said, "An out-of-body experience which I had in 1976 changed my life; it made me more aware of inner images, urgings and intuitions. Since then I have leaned on these aspects of myself when making decisions and life choices." His comments remind us of the opening remarks on wholeness: that wholeness comes to those who find out what is, for them, good and hold fast to that. The peak experience, according to study participants, opens the way to discovery of inner truths and "the good."

The study participants' perception of abundance increased. They speak about experiencing the world around them as luscious and full. They comment how odd it was, given their materially sparse life situations (sparse by their own standards as well as society's), to feel so rich.

This isn't puzzling once we grasp that the peak experience expands our field of consciousness to include everything in the universe: we feel we have everything because we experience Everything within. Maharishi Mahesh Yogi has repeatedly taught that this experience opens the individual up to the "field of all possibilities." This field seems akin to author Joseph Chilton Pearce's "crack in the cosmic egg." Although Pearce is also talking about *metanoia,* the transformation of an individual's entire belief system accompanying the moment of illumination, he writes of the exquisite insight that makes "all things new again." These unifying, integrative moments provide us with a glimpse of the connectivity of all things, the micro/macro web of the universe, interrelationships of all people and things. This way of seeing allows no dualities and shows us we are born, have our lives and "die" within the context of a coherent, comprehensible, intelligent whole—a whole that loses nothing despite its ever changing flux.

As we are lifted out of ourselves, we disconnect from rigid, culturally created laws. We become one with everything, lose our feelings of desperation and feel a deep, healing harmony.

A study participant commented about that healing:

> My transcendent experiences continue to transform my life over and over again, like reverberations that don't end. I've come to accept the fluidity of my life. I'm learning to live a life of faith, trusting I'll be provided for, not in a passive way, of course, but so that fears lessen. My work [i.e., as a result of these experiences] becomes "proving" God in every action, every event, even in life's difficulties. Not I, but Thou. Ultimately, there's nowhere else to turn. Union of this sort, [which I've carried with me since self-transcendence] is healing. What creates insanity is separation.

We who have felt such liberation leave the narrow confines of ordinary waking consciousness. As a result, our energy, intensity, focus and elation are greatly enhanced. For some, this is a once-in-a-lifetime glimpse of what we are at our deepest level of being, a glimpse that changes us forever. For others, these instances repeat. For those of us with a natural propensity toward mysticism (and not all those who have the peak experience possess that leaning) peaking introduces us to infinity. It is our life-altering initiation into the cosmic sense.

Poet, artist and mystic William Blake likened this condition of mind, heart and perception to the *cleansing* of our perceptual field. In his now classic verse from *The Marriage of Heaven* (classic no doubt because his words articulate and frame the ineffable for scores of others to understand), we read:

> If the doors of perception were cleansed, everything would appear to man as it is, infinite. For man has closed himself up, till he sees all thro' the narrow chinks of his cavern.[4]

At the very least, the peak experience widens our perception so that we "see" something larger, so that our creaturely mind fuses itself to the Eternal, Infinite state of consciousness.

Maslow called the peak experience an "acute identity experience." He meant that we become ourselves in a pure and uncontaminated way; that we feel boundless, at one with the world, at peace, simultaneously powerful and vulnerable. For the moment, our logical, culturally conditioned thought processes, our time/space orientation are suspended. Self-consciousness evaporates in a new paradigm of Self-awareness. The individual in the peak experience is always liberated, "free," or some say, enlightened, illumined, full of light. He or she is unconstricted and spontaneous, yet completely focused and totally present.

Maslow believed that the world could be divided into two "religions": peakers and nonpeakers. Of this division, he noted some people can't admit to having had a core or peak experience and subsequently can't use such experiences to further their own development. Believing that these people were constitutionally different, "with a profound characterological makeup" completely at odds with the character structure of peakers, Maslow suggested nonpeakers either deny, repress or perhaps never have had peak experiences. He also proposed that LSD or other similar drugs might stimulate such experiences in nonpeakers, thus closing the gap between these two dissimilar types of humans:

> In the last few years it has become quite clear that certain drugs called "psychedelic," especially LSD and psilocybin, give us some possibility of control in this realm of peak experiences....Perhaps we can actually produce a private personal peak experience under observation and whenever we wish under religious or non-religious circumstances...[thus bridging the gap] between these two separated halves of mankind.[5]

My own observations, which I'll expand on shortly, indicate two primary dangers in this argument. First, long-term effects of psychedelic drugs may actually deprive users of motivation to grow or function in a way that furthers their highest welfare. The effects of such drugs ultimately may render persons so lethargic, if only for a time, that they will not seek out the very experiences, rigorous as these might be, that are needed to confront self-imposed limits in wholesome ways, and thus grow. Second, in my opinion, there is still an unexplained connection between our central nervous system, our individual ability to experience transcendence, and our worldview as a whole. I'm not convinced that the long-range effects of any drugs on our nervous system can produce the effects Maslow hoped for.

Also, as an educator who has seen countless people—children, young adults and adults—at various levels of learning, I find it somewhat intolerant, perhaps even insulting, to require another to take a drug to experience what I value.

Moreover, my professional view about peakers versus non-peakers, at its core, is unlike Maslow's. While I also meet many men and women who do not recall having had a peak experience (denying, repressing or simply not having had them), I sense this lack is itself symptomatic of a phase in the development of consciousness, not a division of *types* of humans, nor evidence that the other is characterologically or constitutionally "different."

This view is in keeping with the Eastern (in this case, Hindu) idea of levels of consciousness. At this time, my conceptual framework, which seems helpful to this issue, goes this way: all humans experience three basic levels or dimensions of consciousness — waking, dreaming and dreamless sleep. The fourth level, pure awareness, what I have been calling God-consciousness, transcendence or the peak experience (and some might say these are different), is gained suddenly during prayer, meditation or through some unexpected grace, epiphany or creative moment. This seems, to me, of grace—not drugs or self-will. The fifth stage, (what Bucke called "cosmic consciousness") is reached when the fourth state of transcendent awareness is *retained* along with the three other, relative states. In chapter 8, one of the case-study interviewees describes this fourth state quite well. The two highest states of consciousness are God-consciousness, wherein the individual experiences ever subtler realms of transcendent thought during ordinary waking and dream states, and finally Unity-consciousness, wherein the individual's nervous system *and* regular consciousness are so highly developed that he or she lives *in* total unity with the Absolute. Dante, Eckhart and certain saints probably could serve as archetypes for these states, although hopefully not in any clinical way.

Each of these states is a logical consequence of the one that precedes it. For instance, the mystic state would flow naturally out of the fourth phase—the transcendent level of consciousness. This framework until recently has been lacking in the Western tradition. It is to me elegant and orderly, especially in terms of understanding religious or peak experiencers and mystics, also known as "contemplatives."

First, under this conceptual system, a peak experiencer is not necessarily a mystic. One who has had a single, or several, peak experiences may not be moved to search for a repeat of the experience. Or to spend an entire life searching for God. Many great artists, athletes, mothers, executives and scientists show the *effects* of self-transcendence (and even, in their comments, acknowledge having had such moments), yet are not moved to do much more than use insights gained to become the best person they can be, within the context of their conventional lives. Does the mystic's desire for oneness with God give him or her a corner on being a "better" person? Or a higher species? One supposes a key is found in the "fruits" of desires, the outcomes of life. Mystics, by definition, dedicate their lives to attaining union with the Transcendent; the peak experience fuels and energizes their desires, while in most others it just enriches, heals and adds more meaning to life.

✭ ✭ ✭

Second, mystics can attain a highly developed cosmic sense and still have a long way to go in behavioral development. Returning to peakers and nonpeakers, my current feeling is that the more highly evolved our consciousness the more likely it is that we will have and remember peak experiences. The more open we will be to such ideas, including the idea of an orderly, abundant universe; the interrelationship of all life; the acceptance of Eternity.

✭ ✭ ✭

In my professional practice I deal primarily with well-educated, bright and ambitious executives (especially creative, entrepreneurial types). I find most are reasonably open to discussing such issues once they trust the person they're speaking to. Even the most linear thinkers, when gently encouraged, recall such experiences, since there are many common life instances that provide access to the peak moment. For example, in sports or when concentrating on a complex, engaging business problem, one works and then relaxes. The subsequent leisure or rest often gives rise to the peak moment, the "aha" experience in which insights about an answer we want pops into mind. Intense focus, present-centeredness, then rest is said to produce answers. Even during a sexual experience, the moment of orgasm is often likened to a peak experience in that the individual "ego" is momentarily dissolved. ★★★

A client, a lawyer with whom I regularly visit (and as bright, ethical and sensitive a man as one could hope to meet), reacted skeptically when I first mentioned my interest in mysticism and peak experiences. He said that he had never had a peak experience. He felt that only "emotional types" cared about such matters. Knowing he was an avid skier, I asked him if, while skiing, he'd ever been so totally absorbed in the activity that he'd forgotten all work, cares and fears. Had he ever entered the skiing with such high absorption that he actually *became* the skiing? He remembered many such experiences, broke out in a big smile and said that he hadn't realized that was what it was. He added that these moments were, for him, the highlights of his life, times of incredible happiness, balance and focus. He commented that during those times he was so fully engrossed that business cares, other worries and goals all seemed to vanish in a sense of tremendous power and freedom.

Whatever our life interests, this is exactly the outcome of the peak experience: we become egoless, perceive a kind of perfection in and around us, and transcend ourselves in a fashion that makes all things whole.

These instances bring us joy—true happiness. We feel justified in some way, as if life has expanded meaning and elegance. Of his skiing episodes, my client said that he always felt renewed afterward, and he wondered if that was why, when he'd had too much of work and pressure, he headed for the ski slopes. When too busy to ski, just remembering his experiences on the slopes refreshed him.

In fact, feelings of renewal often continue long after the peak experience. Transcenders can, and regularly do, enter into the memory of their egoless times whenever they feel the need to be refreshed. Something cleansing, organizing and stress-releasing occurs to the entire mind/body through these experiences. This purification coupled with a cluster of perceptual changes (such as *being* more responsive, holistic and synergistic rather than just *thinking* about these values) contributes greatly to psychic health.

In spite of all the benefits of the illuminative moment described above, the achievement orientation of the Western world has long been closed to this type of experience. The great prophets and seers in every major religion have probably all had a core religious or peak experience. Yet little is said about such matters in the traditional church environment. Almost every Judeo-Christian group has its highly organized, legalistic and dogmatic administrative arm. Within that, a smaller, essentially spiritual worship faction exists. Usually this spiritual core is just a handful of unorganized, disconnected individuals whose prayer life richly contributes to their ability to commune intimately with God. Perhaps they could be called mystics. Perhaps not. These individuals whose spiritual experiences are likely to be revelatory, transcendent, illuminative may belong to any of the great world religions or be isolates, set apart from any religious structure.

Overall, our Western religious culture, with some exceptions— primarily stemming from the Catholic monastic traditions, the more liberal elements within the Episcopal Church, some evangelical or charismatic movements that stress the healing and transformative power of the Holy Spirit, and a few psychoanalytic schools (e.g., Jungian, Assagioli and the Transpersonal Schools, etc.)—remain stubbornly closed to the subject of mysticism and the higher reaches of transpersonal consciousness.

On the macro level of society, our relatively young culture has only recently become sufficiently developed to entertain such ideas. Also, the teaching of the Church after the Middle Ages contributed to a long-lasting negative attitude about mysticism.

During the early period of the Church, through at least the first decade after Christ, the religious traditions encouraged contemplative religious experiences. An intimate, direct relationship with God, an experiential relationship, which I'll assume would have been a level of consciousness open to transcending, was what Saint Paul must have been referring to when he spoke of *knowing* God. His own conversion experience was sudden, and transformed his life's course. After that, Paul frequently urged his disciples to grow in their own intimate knowledge of God.[6]

This positive tradition of the contemplative knowledge of the Absolute continued through the Middle Ages, when medieval monks practiced a somewhat "methodless" prayer: they repeated scriptural passages, listening to their words as they said them, entering into these sacred phrases with their entire minds and bodies. Monks memorized many passages of Scripture since there was no printing, therefore no books. This vocal or subvocal prayer was their life-changing response to God; it represented their direct, meditative discourse with him, as chanting and other liturgical prayers may do today.

Monks and nuns were transported physically and mentally, that is, experientially, rather than just intellectually, into close, intimate communion with God.

During that era prayer, contemplation and meditation were woven together into one undivided communing with God. These three acts could be engaged in during the same prayer session, and frequently resulted in a kind of resting *in* God much as in Eastern meditation where individuals transcend their thought boundaries to unite with the Absolute.

Around the twelfth century, things began to change. With the birth of many new schools of theology and a more precise, analytical approach to prayer and religious practices grew the tendency to classify, analyze and compartmentalize prayer life, and a lessening of contemplative prayer.

The compartmentalization of prayer into different types, the idea that contemplation was reserved for an elite few, that it might even be full of dangers and not something to which the ordinary Christian should aspire, were all factors that eroded mystical theology during the sixteenth and seventeenth centuries:

> The final nail that was hammered into the coffin of the traditional teaching of the Church was the obvious corollary that it was against humility to aspire to contemplation.... As devout people moved spontaneously into [the normal contemplative view of truth during prayer] they were up against this very negative attitude. They hesitated to go beyond discursive meditation because of instructions or warnings they were given about the dangers of mysticism. They either gave up mental prayer altogether, or, through the mercy of God, found some way of persevering in spite of the obstacles.[7]

This brief overview could explain why there's been a general inattention, if not outright skepticism, to the positive potentials inherent in the mystic consciousness. When Maslow and others codified the benefits of the peak experience as well as the Being-values (i.e., values that correspond to the awareness of the transcendent realm), the clergy, researchers, educators and various other helping professions began paying closer attention to the attitudes, behaviors and values of psychic health. As I've mentioned periodically, the helping professions in my observation and experience are still tied too closely, in their own awareness and training, to psychic deficits: to fear, phobias, syndromes, limits, the "coping" needs of human beings who manufacture or are at the effect of their own problems and narcissisms. Their modality of advice giving, their frame of reference and professional biases encourage "adjusting" to a culturally defined reality, a set of problems not geared to introducing people to their transpersonal, higher selves. Of course, this is a generality. There is a new wave of psychologists, physicians and other health-care professionals concerned with wellness, spiritually conscious choice, ⋆ responsible action. They seem still in the minority, surrounded by peers who by their own perceptions present a limited set of options to their clients and patients.

As we have seen, some authors (such as Underhill and Bucke) have suggested that only the mystic can be called whole, awakened to the hidden powers of an otherwise sleeping self. That may be true. As described, the experience of awakening profoundly impacts an individual's well-being, self-view and the expression of the best self.

However, awakening the "sleeping self" could have a drawback. People who stretch the limits of their consciousness, and thus their nervous systems, may experience psychological and even physical discomfort.

During much of the early stages of the mystic path, the psyche moves sporadically toward an ever higher, expanded consciousness.

As individuals push into newly developed, unexplored and highly private experience, at the very least, they tap tender emotions. They can feel inordinately sad, vulnerable or irritable with little or no provocation.

One man told me that during a meeting, for no apparent reason, some heroic quality in a colleague so moved him that he had to fight back tears. Another said that he'd had long periods when he couldn't socialize, so intense was his need for solitude, privacy and quiet. Yet another reported feeling vulnerable, with feelings much like she'd had when her child was born and she didn't want other people approaching her baby. She said, "I feel very tender inside, as if I want to protect myself against negativity, smallness of mind, as if I'm incubating something within.... I intuitively know this [vulnerability] won't last, but right now I have a lot of difficulty being with people."

★ ★ ★

The Western tradition, our schools, social institutions, helping professionals, our training support systems and even churches and synagogues have little empathy for solitude. The "togetherness" banner waves over every social institution: individuals are taught that they must marry; families are taught they must do everything together; marriages are built on the foundation of constant time together (with few options for either spouse to spend time alone, as if solitude was a mark of a failing marriage); children are encouraged to socialize continually, "tested" by therapists when they don't and getting very little encouragement or practice in spending time alone. Corporations (a set of systems I'm very familiar with) are often punitive with those who want to spend time by themselves (lunches, coffee breaks, dinners out are all considered times to socialize with others). Our whole cultural setup is geared to interactive games. Little wonder that when individuals start to grow spiritually or develop an intuitive, spiritual intelligence, they may find it necessary to retreat, pull back and learn how to be alone.

Moreover, the Western tradition has few role models for those encountering the turmoils of inner growth. Even though common sense tells us that whenever any of us extend ourselves into the farther reaches of our awareness, awakening to what is deepest and most sacred within—with our unique psyche, dream images, memories, aspirations—we may suffer a subtle, even devastating, level of unexplainable stress. I call this stress "extension stress," and define it as the wear and tear within the psyche of one who is reaching toward new levels of awareness *and* functioning.

Really, this is only an adjustment of the definition of "distress" researcher Hans Selye gave us many years ago. Extension stress can be compared to the stresses suffered by those rare Olympic athletes who push their minds and bodies to the outer limits, that their physical performances might scale new heights. With such goals they must convince themselves that their body *can* do what they demand. The person who desires self-transcendence, who spends long hours in meditation, reflection, prayer for spiritual rebirth faces change, even a good deal of pain. Pain might come from any number of sources: from the birth of new sensibilities, from reflecting on one's entire life (including the refinement of habits, behaviors, relationships) and from letting go, as described in previous chapters, of culturally ingrained ideas, possessions, aspirations. Initially, letting go is loss. All loss carries with it grief work, and stresses that take time to work through, and questions about existential choices, the consequences of which may be unpalatable.

One who starts this work from the vantage point of an Eastern tradition has a time-honored and more detailed developmental road map to follow. There are gurus, teachers, myths, techniques, symbolism and a language that makes the pain of spiritual transitions understandable. However, in the West, with our emphasis on competition, social and personal gratification and a psychoanalytic, parenting and educational tradition that encourages "adjustment" rather than actualization (actualization is often interpreted as "Me-ism"), there is a strong tendency to view psychic turmoil (especially that which comes from the inner journey) as neurotic or selfish or hypochondriacal.

Fortunately, increasing attention is being given to thinkers who acknowledge the difficulties faced by those undergoing this most sincere and radical transformation. Thomas Merton sug-

gests that an existential anxiety crisis precedes the final integration of life as a "new man."[8] He tells us that this is a necessary
partner to psychic rebirth, our birth into a higher level of functioning, perceiving, feeling. Final integration, because it demands
a state of functioning and maturity beyond mere "adjustment,"
creates the cosmic or universal man:

> He has gained a deeper, fuller identity than that of his
> limited ego-self which is only a fragment of his
> being....He has attained to a deep inner freedom—the
> Freedom of the Spirit we read about in the New
> Testament....Now, this calls to mind the theology of
> St. Thomas on the Gifts of the Holy Spirit which move
> a man to act in a "superhuman mode."[9]

The crisis we face while en route to that transfiguration is
often more distressing than those born of ordinary life. Saint John
of the Cross felt that any separation from God was like a "dark
night." He passed through a period of intense discomfort—feeling
troubled; resisting his spiritual work; feeling as if "devils" were
assaulting him at every turn. Merton suggests that anyone undergoing final integration would (if "discovered") soon find him- or
herself getting shock treatments designed to effectively take care
of any further "disturbing" developments.

One of the study participants described his own "dark
night" this way:

> I was bereft, having started on a path I knew nothing
> about. I'd left all my old friends, key members of my
> family, felt totally alone. I could remember flashes of
> experiences where I'd felt at one with the Absolute.
> Those experiences had encouraged me in a way no
> social or material accomplishment ever had. Yet I was
> cut off even from those experiences. I felt I had no

options, not one way to go that could help; not even suicide was open to me, believing as I do that when you take your own life you'll have unresolved issues to deal with at another time, in another way. All I could do was wait. The waiting, painful as it was, disturbed as I was, strengthened me, deepened my faith. I found in my waiting that the demands placed upon me prompted a response from me, that my own responding to life's demands was a source of hope for me. That was really all I had: my ability to respond. But it helped me through a most difficult time. My own response deepened my faith.

The language of some faiths offers us sacred terms for spiritual growth, such as "the self," "spiritual death," and "death followed by the reintegration of the social-self." During this period it is inner solitude, loneliness, perhaps despair, that create the emotional and often the physical ills of depression that society so poorly understands and cannot tolerate.

The Eastern tradition has always acknowledged that the rebirth process (including self-annihilation and the reintegration of personality) is painful. The Zen tradition, for example, in keeping with its rather intellectual observer's stance relative to attachment, acknowledges such pain. Yet it may instruct followers to detach from mental discomfort as well as pleasure as just something else to relinquish on the path to *satori*.

Hindu schools talk of *kundalini*, described earlier as an energy residing (or sleeping) at the base of the spine that begins its awakening move when the individual starts the rebirth process through selected meditative techniques. According to believers, when this energy awakens it can create havoc in the central nervous system, until it works its way up the spinal column, removing all blocks and stresses as it goes. This belief seems a legacy, a sort of rite of passage, for spiritual growth, and a conceptual framework for the rebirth process that could help integrate spiritual experience.

Gopi Krishna, who charted his experiences in his autobiography, *Kundalini,* describes one incident in which the *kundalini* was moving in his body. He thought he was going to die:

> The heat [from the fiery currents that darted through my body] grew every moment, causing such unbearable pain that I writhed and twisted from side to side while streams of cold perspiration poured down my face and limbs. But still the heat increased....Suffering the most excruciating torture...there were dreadful disturbances in all the organs, each so alarming and painful that I wonder how I managed to retain my self-possession....The whole delicate organism was burning, withering away completely under the fiery blast racing through its interior.[10]

Western medicine is slow to realize that a mere change in thought can affect the physical body, for better or worse. It has "discovered" that the brain, as the largest gland in the body, emits specific hormones depending on the type of idea thinkers hold, that ideas are "things" in the body, with the power to create life or death. Is it surprising that people who consciously choose to disintegrate their old selves—egocentricity, cultural conditioning—and who risk the challenges of solitary life during a period of psychic disintegration, might undergo emotional and even physical crisis?

I am, at this writing, unable to explain some of the phenomena I have witnessed (in the study participants and in myself) as clearly as I might wish. For example, in those who have used psychedelic drugs to induce peak experiences I have observed indecisiveness or passivity. One study participant compared this to "living in glue." This observation, seen frequently, gives rise to my earlier conservative stance about the use of drugs to create peak experiences. In these persons, the nervous system seems blocked, robbed of energy, over- or understimulated in a way that creates *inaction* and inability to decide which way to go in a host of simple life choices. What one man described as lethargy may simply be his body's specific response to the type of transformation he desires: radical inner growth, reintegration. In his case, it is likely that energy once available for work, social relations and creative effort is now redirected toward exploring the frontiers of consciousness at previously unexamined levels. On the other hand, it could be that the man's nervous system is exhausted, overtaxed either because of drugs or because he hasn't yet adapted to the new faculty of consciousness being sought. I should add that I've also seen people "grow out of" that apathy, eventually returning to more self-expressive, active states, what they call "normal functioning." Clearly, this issue needs added examination, research and clarification.

Our society needs physicians sympathetic to this inquiry: physicians who can help humanity understand the physiology of transcendence; and guides, clerics, counselors, therapists who know something about the "final," integrative phase of self realization; and professionals who know, firsthand, about the rebirth and transpersonal maturity that self-transcendent individuals seek. Too many therapists, psychoanalysts and physicians are either unfamiliar with, or unfriendly toward, spiritual topics, tend to see everything as pathology or treat every problem as disease. Similarly, our Judeo-Christian tradition, unlike the various Eastern schools mentioned, has not been inclined to depend on spiritual masters or teachers for human development needs. Perhaps this is a blessing in disguise; certainly we do not need yet another institutionalized tier of experts and new sets of rules, certificates and courses to assist people with what is basically a highly individualized matter.

With all that's been said about our society needing to sensitize itself to the spiritual dimension of life, it's obvious that great geniuses, mystics and saints—(e.g.,Walt Whitman, William Blake, Mother Teresa, Buckminster Fuller and countless others)—have had the clarity and inner resources to foster their own growth in spite of obstacles. However, we could encourage many more ordinary people toward healthier self-development, toward self-transcendence, if schools, churches and other social institutions were simply sympathetic to its values. For people to discover that life is more than "making do," more than adjustment to the expectations of others, society must place as much emphasis on wholesome spiritual growth as it now places on other aspects of individual accomplishment—sports or business prowess, affluence, celebrity.

8

The Mystic's Consciousness: Three Case Studies

Q. If you were to describe to another the attributes that have helped you to be happy, productive and contributive, what would you say these were?

A. Acceptance. Creativity. Perseverance. Inspiration. Hunger for the Divine.

Study participant, California

The following case studies represent three examples of mystic consciousness. These adults meet many, if not all, of the criteria of the mystic described earlier. Each has a decided "hunger for the Divine." Each has an ability to have, recall and use his or her peak experiences. Each continues to grow in the mystic sense, while expressing several key attributes of mysticism: the sense of interrelatedness to all life and the universe; the loss of fears and need for "things"; and compassionate love.

Each one speaks of, and to a great extent, exhibits the cosmic or unitive consciousness explored in the last two chapters. Each perceives daily life as lived in an integrated, "friendly" world, having either totally or partially extinguished the fear of death—as well as other nameless fears that torment most people. Each is functioning effectively, self-sufficiently, in a role natural to his or her own talents, while simultaneously retaining the Transcendent in consciousness.

The first case study, that of a researcher and bibliographer, demonstrates the ongoing yearning, the heart hunger and absorption with the Absolute that are characteristic of the true mystic.

The second case, a housewife and mother, demonstrates the goal-less, nonstriving nature of the completed or actualizing person. She experiences herself as needing nothing more to be happy, as needing no "added thing" for fulfillment. I particularly liked this interview because the study participant expresses a fully rounded happiness that contradicts a standard expectation of many professionals in the mental-health field. (I recall one lecture I heard recently where the speaker, a psychologist and minister, told the audience that adults always feel incomplete, that few could feel satisfied with life, could be goal-less. This sort of misinformation deprives people of hope and models for real joy.)

The third case study, of a writer and poet, illustrates the fully actualizing mystic type with its artistic, intense temperament and aesthetic, passionate interest in spiritual matters, its strongly marked, intimate experience of and relationship to God. It was gratifying to meet this participant, particularly because most of the texts about enlightenment make it seem as though the enlightened individual is a rarity, someone who must travel to far-off lands or study for years and years with gurus in the "outer court" in order to grow self-realized. The participant's comments and—more than that—his utter simplicity of manner and lifestyle, his totally unassuming environment, words, way of seeing things lets each of us see that self-realization, self-transcendence, spiritual "actualization" can be ours; it may be a grace, but it can be ours.

One individual is an active member of an organized religion. The other two, though highly spiritual and sensitive to godly issues, are not churchgoers; if anything, they are like so many of the study participants: turned off to organized religion. As one of the study participants put it, "You can't organize the Truth."

I interpret that reluctance to participate in, or perhaps even relate to, organized religion much as Maslow does: through the

ages, the mystic's experience occurs individually, not institution-
ally, not legitimized by an organized, corporate body. Maslow
pointed out that religious organizations often spring up around
(and are designed to structure, communicate and legitimize) the
illumination, or conversion, experience of one individual. How
difficult for the true mystic to find rapport within such institutions; his or her own heightened sensitivities to God are made
profane by the spiritually immature perceptions of those who
want to hear about, but who themselves do not *experience*, the
sacred reverence and humility of the Transcendent.

At the same time, those who are spiritually inclined, who
belong to and support an organized religion, when attending
church regularly as a result of self-transcendence, seem to
become more devout, more strengthened in their faith. I suspect
that these are highly individualized patterns, that each mystically
inclined individual experiences the Absolute in his or her own
way, much as revelation itself is highly unpredictable and individual.

Each case study is presented with a slightly different
emphasis; my conversation and correspondence with each individual was one-of-a-kind, taking shape from the participants'
interests and direction. In a manner typical to my professional
practice, in which I interview many people each week, I joined
the study participants where they were, that is, entered their
world, their reality, rather than asking them to join me in mine.
In one case, the first, I had to interview the participant over the
phone; our phone conversations were followed by his several letters to me. I met the others at their homes for a lengthy in-person
talk. Fortunately, each is articulate, a patient teacher, easy to
understand.

Case Study #1
Researcher, Bibliographer (Male)

The first participant lives in the South as a "hermit in the woods." He is in his fifties, and left suburbia when his wife, now deceased, and his sons began looking for a wilderness site on which to live. His small cabin has no utilities, no running water. He runs his mail-order business largely by battery-operated computers. He wrote in one letter. "I go 'out' three times a week, enjoy the solitude, and try (not always efficiently) to conduct my business as a service for people looking for inaccessible books."

Of his own growth, solitary life and work he said:

"For years I was unconsciously seeking approval from other people, wanting them to tell me I'm all right. Now I see that this sort of assurance is irrelevant, even if it were possible to get: that in assuming others were 'all right' but being uncertain of myself, my misunderstanding of them was as complete as my misunderstanding of myself. In truth I wasn't all right; no one's sanction could change this.

"So what happened? Within the bounds of respectability, I developed some goals (which are still before me), but made a string of botched attempts at life, including my working life."

[Note: he says his "larger Self" is now able to comment with openness on the fearfulness of his previous "small self," without inordinate need to defend himself, a sign that his fears and sense of inadequacy are dissolving.]

"For living, solitude is perhaps best for me; for work, my computer is the effective solution. Regarding work, I've lived all my life with books.... I've now realized the extensive monograph and lists that I've accumulated has potential to be of great help to others.

"It's much more difficult to write about life. Basically, we do not see the whole picture. From birth we perceive it through the gates of our physical senses and are taught to instill those responses which are culturally 'correct.' It is hard work to question those imposed interpretations about reality and attempt to establish our own. Two key insights I'm reaching involve change and death: we are temporary, in process; and we shall die. Accordingly, we can see and touch nothing that is fixed, changeless, absolute. First, one realizes that everything is relative, maybe later on that everything is related....From here it is a short step to developing a sense of stewardship: I have the responsibility of caring for what is entrusted to me and of limiting my acquisitions of more than I need.

"It is an illusion to suppose that any security can be found on earth: the only security is trust in God....After half a century and much struggle to discern, I believe that to be true of the human situation. Much of the disorder that we see in others comes from confused priorities and from attempts to be in control."

[Note: here he illustrates the growing sense of interrelatedness, stewardship born of love and identification with the other-as-self.]

"I'm slowly learning that other people are basically like me. I can assume that the deep 'self' of another will answer [in kind] (if able to respond freely) whenever I expect to discover a brother or sister. These discoveries affirm a [spiritual] depth in me and reinforce my growing sense of who people are.

"...the only adequate answer I know is that we are all being called to become brothers and sisters in Christ."

Of his experience with self-transcendence, he noted:

"My earliest spiritual experience was when I was about fifteen and saw Van Gogh's *Crows over a Cornfield* in an exhibition. I was transfixed and lost all sense of time. I learned years later that he painted this just before shooting himself. Another experience was [what I call my] 'foot of the cross' experience about eight years ago."

[Note: the following passage exemplifies the apparent ease with which most mystics can enter the transcendent realm. This man spontaneously "used" external stimuli and his own, made-up exercises to transcend, as well as having had previous experiences on which to draw.]

"The 'foot of the cross' exercise is a spiritual process of sorts, in which I imaginatively place myself at the foot of the cross, and then a sense of deep humility comes to me as I realize that God is present. I don't exactly think back to specific transcendent situations; the spiritual exercises serve as that reminder. By knowing these have occurred, I can let them happen again.

"I find these extremely helpful and fruitful to me, to my development. These spiritual exercises are quite simple actually, yet profound enough to result in a kind of dropping of barriers. I join a reality which is for me healing and, as in the 'foot of the cross' exercise, humbling.

"Now just thinking of those exercises…transports me to that cluster of feelings which accompanied the original experience."

Of his ongoing spiritual study and "place" along the path, he described his thoughts and readings in typically abstract language:

"I am reading and studying C. F. Kelly on Meister Eckhart and find it helpful to my growth. A deep comparison of Saint Francis with Meister Eckhart would be splendid, as they complement each other. A fusion might resemble Jesus."

Case Study #2
Housewife and Mother

This woman lives in a spacious, contemporary home overlooking the Pacific Ocean. The house sits near a cliff on an open meadow. It is orderly and neat. Apart from the sound of the ocean and the humming motor of a huge fish tank with tropical fish, the house is silent.

The study participant has been married for twenty-some years, has two children, and with the exception of teaching a Yoga class once each week for the last eight years, her primary occupation is being a wife and mother.

Of her homemaking role and life's philosophy, she said:

"What makes life meaningful to me is something beautiful to see, hear or smell every day. Something to look forward to. A sense of being a positive force in someone else's life, for example, my husband's or child's or a friend's life. I feel I'm creative when I establish a pleasant atmosphere for my family to relax and enjoy *their* lives.

"I've been married for twenty years, through good and not-so-good times, and have kept it a good relationship. I've always been here when my children needed me, and I try to set a good example with my behavior and philosophy.

"I've come to the point in my life where I don't attend social gatherings unless it's really necessary. This came about by my feeling a sense of time wasted when I found myself talking about meaningless things, after a while, I noticed my mind just drifting away from these kinds of conversations. Negative, judgmental attitudes of many people were depressing to me. Now, although a large part of my day is spent planning family meals and taking care of the house, I have more time to enjoy the things I like (one of which is *not* cooking!). I stay on top of housework so that it never gets out of hand, never piles up to be a big job. I keep our debts to a minimum. I eat and exercise properly so that there is no worry about health, and I follow something disliked with something nice."

[Note: Here we see the ease with which the individual adopts self-discipline, doing for others and a willingness to simplify life. Her remark about feeling a sense of wasted time when in superficial social situations was typical for most of those in the study, all of whom were quick to abandon "meaningless" activities.]

"Relatives wonder why I don't visit them when I'm in their area. Friends wonder at my difficulty in holding a train of thought when I'm around them in social gatherings. Once, for example, a friend confessed to me that he had to 'explain' my husband (who is also a private person) and me to his friends.

"This is fine with me. I have no need for approval from others for my thinking and way of being. I don't mind being thought of as weird. I enjoy being alone.

"If I'm ever down, if life ever seems to lack meaning for me, I take a long walk. I notice all the little things: microscopic flowers, insects, bark, spider webs, birdsongs, water dripping, pine cones popping. I've done that ever since I was a child, and it always opens me up to a wonderful feeling. I believe that if things don't turn out the way I want, it's because there's a better way up ahead. I've gotten everything I've ever wanted, and some things I only thought I wanted. So I feel very lucky in all respects, and very happy too. There's really nothing I need or want to be happy. I am fulfilled right now."

About her peak experiences and ability to communicate these to her family:

"I experience these episodes of great happiness, a welling up of joy or ecstasy inside myself about two or three times per week; very frequently now. My husband might reject everything I say about these things, but when I see him over in the living room I think he's testing out some meditation technique, trying to get to this place in consciousness that I've been describing to him. Of course, when I ask him what he's doing, he says to me, 'I'm resting.' And, I just leave it at that.

"My son, however, has similar experiences to mine. He's quite dyslexic, and I'm beginning to think that there's something about that physical state that may prompt transcending. I read that Einstein was dyslexic and told my son that, and he seemed to like having a connection with Einstein.

"Once my son had a fever; he was just a little boy then. He left his body during that fevered state: he got so scared. He was crying for me, and when I came in he was in tears, saying that he was in a corner of the room. About the same time, after he was well of course, he began to see the aura around flowers. He's very sensitive, very much like me. I'd say he's developed in this area since then. He was around seven then, and he's further along now as a result of those early experiences. ★-★-★

"He likes to walk as I do, and see all the little life—the tiny flowers and insects and ways of nature."

About her life-goals she added:

"Maybe I don't need to have a goal. I really don't know if I have any more goals. To have a goal means you have to pick a spot you want to reach eventually. That takes the fun out of it for me. I just try to have a little fun each day, enjoy every day for itself. I like the spot I'm in, right here and right now.

"I have a perfect life. I don't feel I have to work toward a perfect life; it's already here for me.

"As for some of the larger social movements, like Women's Lib, that doesn't touch me. I've always felt liberated. I've never had to compete in the working field because my work has been to be a wife and mother. Also, I'd like to say that I have no fear of aging whatsoever, no fear of death. I feel immortal."

Case Study #3
Writer/Poet (Male)

This man currently lives in his own studio "space," a single, neatly furnished room in the home of a family of friends. He is in his thirties and has a tidy, focused appearance. His room is immaculate, somewhat sparsely furnished except for a huge number of books and a rather cluttered writing table full of papers and reference works. The studio overlooks a forest meadow; beyond it, about two miles away, is the Pacific Ocean.

The study participant is single, a college graduate who now writes poetry and also teaches self-development seminars (i.e., about subjects similar to the themes of this book). He notes that, to his best recollection, his mystic interests started developing at about the age of twenty-nine due to certain drug-induced peak experiences:

"These opened me up to nature, punctured a shield of some sort. Thereafter aesthetics, history, the physical earth and sciences were blended for me. I felt completely related to everything. These experiences 'purified' my perception, although I felt originally in a sort of 'dark night' process in which I was lost. As I look back on that period I see it was a beginning point for me, not an ending. It was a start of that which I now call 'sympathetic magic,' in which disbelief and doubt are suspended. These experiences are what opened me up to my own inner promptings."

Of his peak experiences, he said this:

"There is a unity consciousness in these times for me, an experience which has nothing to do with time, a wholeness felt concretely. I can be picking out lenses for a camera or doing something quite mundane, or even be in a problem-solving mode, and I'm never *not* in that [wholeness] space.

"I call this a 'silent space' period, an intensity that is functioning within me while I'm in activity. For example, I can be in a highly active situation, with others, and feel quiet space within me. Or I can be alone and be anything *but* quiet inside. This space within, for want of a better phrase, is also something that allows me to see that in a time of trouble I can have very positive results.

It's as if I'm totally guided from within now, and thus always perfectly directed.

[Note: in the previous comments and those that follow, we hear of the ease with which he "enters" the Transcendent, as do our other two study participants. In this man's case, however, the Absolute remains in consciousness for what apparently are long stretches of time. Also, in a similar sounding way to the second participant, we hear the same nonstriving attitude, although here we find the goal-less way of being is quite active in the world. Again, this participant tells us about the difficulty of being with others whose worldview and consciousness are not aligned to the Absolute.]

"It's a strange thing, but when you have this wholeness you have everything. It's strengthening. When this energy is there, ultimately what you need isn't material. You need very little. I mean I can live with practically nothing now. The challenge that remains is other people's values; their consciousness. But the bedrock within me is wholeness."   ✭✭✭

As for intimacy, he said:

"You cannot have a true relationship without having that space developed within you because with it you can stand alone, so now you can *choose* a relationship. Everything, even my ability to relate to others, to be truthful to them and to myself, comes from this bedrock of silence within.

"In terms of goals, I no longer think it's a question of 'my' wanting anything. The energy in me, that which I call the 'bedrock of wholeness,' dictates what happens next. If I get receptive enough to it, if I get sympathetic enough, I hear the words being shaped within me; through my *being* I am shaped. There is, however, a simultaneity to this: it's not a question of me or It; we are one. The one becomes two and then...then it sort of takes on a third, to make it whole. This is difficult to describe. The third element is a state, is the basis of the oneness, is inseparable from 'That.' From this third I am open to All in All."

[Note: in the next passage, he describes how his feelings of separateness have all but disappeared, reminding us of 2 Corinthians 3:18, "We shall be completely transformed and changed into God," the goal of all true mystics. Moreover, in previous comments this participant reflects the more fully developed mystic's stance, as did the housewife and mother before him, of needing nothing because he has it all. Not only that, but in his case we hear understanding; the certainty that the two, the Transcendent and himself are one. Again, in the following words about fragmentation and separation, the theme of oneness returns.]

"Now I see that fragmentation is what separates us. There is no separation in truth, not when one is whole inside. The meaning is in life, life itself is the meaning. That silence, that whole, that bedrock within, that's the meaning, energy and purpose of it all. Nothing else is needed. Epiphany, to me, is opening up to that space."

Of his own life-journey, his life-transition, he said:

"I see that in the last two or three years I've changed. I've always had a place separate from others. Even when I was in a major relationship, I've been in the world but not of it, always somewhat detached. It is a recent development for me that I can be with others, with large numbers of people, and when with them, I am still in a sea of silence. I carry that with me. As a result, I now am balancing the two: relatedness and isolation— more than ever before."

Of his present life and daily schedule, he added:

"I do have a discipline: it's a sort of walking meditation, Yoga meditation, in which I become mindful as I walk, and during my daily, rather lengthy walks, find that I integrate my stillness into my activity."

[Note: this is similar, in practice, to the woman who talked about the wonderful feeling she entered when she went for a walk, attending, during her walk, to all the "little things" around her. That mindfulness, as the Easterners might call it, is apparently something each enters into quite naturally, as a self-designed device to invite Transcendent consciousness.]

"I've always been interested in monastic life, and never had it in my head to do much else. That priority set the ground around my activities, and I suppose I had the attributes for that too. I'd say my characteristics set the focus for me. But lately, as I've already mentioned, I'm seeing a change toward new activities. I'm doing so many things now which I'd never even thought about before.

"In the past, I've found it an obstacle to juggle my inner needs with the material, practical and survival issues of life. Now I see that when the right energy is there, there are very few obstacles remaining. My work is my life, is my play, is my being in the world.

"You asked what Christ means to me. I'd answer that there are certain people who appear to have a path, who follow it with intensity. He had a resonance which exemplified God. Mother Teresa has a handle like that.

"You also asked if I ever go to church. I'm never not in church."

PART THREE
The Way of Wholeness

Mention is made of two classes of yogis: hidden and the known. Those who have renounced the world are the "known" yogis: all recognize them. But the "hidden" yogis live in the world. They are not known.

Sri Ramakrishna, *The Gospel of Sri Ramakrishna*

It is not to be learned by world-flight, running away from things, turning solitary and going apart from the world. Rather, one must learn an inner solitude, wherever or with whomsoever he may be.

Raymond Bernard Blakney
Meister Eckhart: A Modern Translation

9

The Look of Wholeness

> Calmness of mind does not mean you should stop
> your activity. Real calmness should be found in activ-
> ity itself. Ram Dass[1]

As the study participants express, actualizing individuals
grow in self-awareness, develop a firm identity and become
guided by interior truths; ultimately they grow keenly receptive
to what is, for them, real and worthwhile, as well as to what is
superfluous or dishonest. It is this knowledge and the actions
flowing from it that help them make a radical break with ordinary
life—*not* necessarily the location in which they live, or an occupation, or economic or marital status, or any other mechanical
aspect of life and self-expression. The transformation is deeper.

When speaking of social and self-transcendence we are talking primarily of that life-movement that is tending toward
authenticity. The individual is shedding rigid, false attitudes, culturally imposed beliefs and illusions. Be assured that such shedding cannot be identified by how life "looks" externally. No mood
making, postures of saintliness, no overt acts of charity qualify us
as authentic. The point of that genuineness, as was pointed out
in the first section of this book, is this: that whoever finds out
what is, at the heart, good and virtuous and holds fast to it
becomes whole.

This is a significant issue in self-development; the progression of finding and expressing one's "good" cannot be equated
with narcissism or hedonism. When I refer to "an individual's
good" I mean those traits, values and qualities that reflect one's
root of humanity, individuality, one's truest self. The entire

process of expressing that good requires us to set standards for our entire life. It means knowing what is worth living for, as well as what is worth dying for. It means learning how to positively rebel against our own unconscious living, our slavish responses, as well as against those things—however innocent and warming in society—that ask us to silence our dignity, our nobility. The study participants' remarks may lead some readers to think that a physical break with conventional life is necessary in order to become actualized. Nothing could be further from the truth.

While the participants represent vivid examples of the progression of actualizing, they do not have a corner on that market. *How* someone lives (i.e., lifestyle, whether one is a parent or not, where one resides, the material goods one keeps or gives away, etc.) is less relevant to wholeness than *who* one is, what one values, chooses, sacrifices, loves as an individual.

The goal of social and self-transcendence is to "be in the world, but not of it," to use a scriptural injunction. Detachment from the world's ideal of "good" or "proper" is an absolute requisite for being and becoming one's own. Detachment does not mean withdrawal. Nor does it mean those common types of nonconformity that people use to protest society's ills: vain adjustments of dress or diet; neurotic self-involvements; psychosomatic or, worse, the psychotic, perhaps even criminal, antisocial or insane acts that poison everything touched. These futile attempts to voice frustration and stand out as a person are not only misdirected but also inept, and inadequately satisfy the potent, positive growth process under discussion: wholeness, as we see, means fruitful.

By detachment I mean an objectivity that allows us to live productively within society while at the same time becoming centered in that "bedrock of wholeness," as one study participant called the higher Self—his, and society's, highest good. This objectivity seems requisite to knowing *what is* good, as well as knowing when we are being swayed, intimidated or even angered by conventional directives. Few want to develop that level of detachment; it requires giving up the security of being "adjusted," requires, ultimately, that we *act* on behalf of what we identify as good.

Almost all of us believe that we must adjust to the world, that this adjustment makes for health, happiness and appropriate living among our neighbors, and even more importantly, that adjustments make for sound mental health. As mentioned, the healthiest of our species apparently take "adjustment" into their own hands, decide for themselves to what they will and will not pay homage.

Decades ago, psychiatrist Robert Lindner wrote about the dangers of blind adjustment. He outlined the natural tension between society's need for order, structure and predictability and the individual's inherent drive to express what is most sacred within. To Lindner, the word "adjustment" was the "theme of our swan song," the idea by which we kill our own will and thwart our spirit:

> You must adjust...this is the motto inscribed on the walls of every nursery, and the process that breaks the spirit are initiated there....Slowly and subtly, the infant is shaped to the prevailing pattern, his needs for love and care turned against him as weapons to enforce submission. Uniqueness, individuality, difference— these are viewed with horror, even shame, at the very least they are treated like diseases, and a regiment of specialists are available today to "cure" the child who will not or cannot conform.[2]

Independent, whole people are often perceived as rule breakers, as standing apart. In fact, they may simply be guilty of detached, creative thinking. They look at things in fresh, unconventional ways. I have written extensively about the problems independent thinkers face in industry[3] and need not dwell on the individual versus society issue here. Suffice it to say that, initially, actualizing individuals (who dare to act on behalf of their insights and truths) may appear to be rebels. This is particularly true in the early stages of social transcendence, when breaking old, habituated responses. Eventually, particularly as wholeness gets established, these individuals *serve* society. They have no choice but to serve, because in actualizing they come to view society, others, as self; discern the interrelatedness of part to whole, understand that what each does makes up the quality and tone of society.

Here is the irony: that we become good stewards to society through the very uniqueness and distinctiveness society would have us snuff out through the "adjustment" it demands.

In these final chapters we leave the study participants to review their lifestyles and organize their comments to see what we can learn about increasing our *own* uniqueness and individuality.

Diverse lifestyles permitted the men and women interviewed in these pages to obtain social and self-transcendence. Some live alone. Others structure solitary time into their married, parental, occupational and recreational lives by eliminating undesirable activities and by streamlining how they manage time, money and their attention. Social and self-transcendence is an ageless, genderless and transcultural phenomenon. Anyone, of any age and background, can grow whole. One only needs a sincere heart and the purity and strength of intent to identify, then express, what is discerned to be true and virtuous.

As a group the study participants have presented themselves as possessing three distinct skills. I am convinced these are the hallmarks of health and the capacity to grow. I call these qualities "skills" because they can be learned, developed, then used on behalf of life. Furthermore, these traits are also aptitudes; they may be, to some extent, natural endowments, yet anyone can cultivate these qualities for greater psychic health.

First, they are *autonomous and authentic.* Each has a high enough self-esteem to be able to act on behalf of what is deemed true and worthwhile. Each has self-trust and self-reliance, knows what is meaningful, can identify, perhaps speak up for and choose, what is valuable and worth aspiring to. These men and women have the necessary energy, determination and resourcefulness to assertively choose and shape a life they find worth living.

It takes self-respect, high self-esteem and self-trust to sacrifice collective opinion, security, customs, guarantees in favor of that which one prefers and thinks best. To sacrifice safe, direct routes of accomplishment, maybe even accomplishment itself as conventionally defined, requires inner strength and faith. By eliminating excessive distractions (for example, socializing, which many said no longer appealed to them), by scaling down debt, possessions and obligations, the study participants demonstrate what sorts of sacrifices they felt compelled to make on behalf of their growth.

The group as a whole possesses *adaptability.* None was so rigidly tied to one course of action or to one narrow belief system that he or she couldn't adjust to environmental pressures or changes. Those who gave up urban living for rural lifestyles and who learned to live without electricity or other modern conveniences; those whose income was decreased by their self-styled lives of "voluntary simplicity"; those who demonstrated increasing ability to rid their life of hypocrisies, who said "goodbye" to toxic relationships or acted against something in their community they felt unjust, unfair (no matter how painful such goodbyes or actions were emotionally) show us why adaptability is a prerequisite to wholesome growth. If we cannot survive without old habits, toxic friendships, addictions, whatever they might be, we are not free to choose our good. And while in the early stages of choosing that good, there is much to endure that calls for adaptability.

Lastly, and each of these characteristics houses a cluster of other traits, aptitudes and skills, the study participants illustrate what it means to be *intuitive.* By becoming more capable of listening to their inner voice, each also reaps rich subjective rewards: knowledge gained from the deepest self, the nonlogical, nonrational self, wisdom that shapes life. Whether gaining intuition through prayer, contemplation, study, walks in the woods or just time spent alone gazing out a window, study participants spoke about receiving insights, feelings and promptings from within. These awarenesses proved to be tremendously healing, helpful to growth, life-choices and informing them they were on the right path, albeit frequently a stony one. More importantly than that inner guidance may be the fact that each is *open to*, responsive to his or her interior "voice," however faint. A complete idea of what life can and should be, what course life can and should take, is emerging.

Factors such as whether an individual is married or single, working or retired, wealthy or poor, in business or barely making ends meet are immaterial to the quest for wholeness. Essential, however, is that the individual designs life so as to grow in awareness, gain strength to respond truthfully, effectually and ethically to daily life—work and relational demands. "Truthful" responses may be exactly opposite to that which others expect and want. That is one goal of wholeness, one reason the adjustment issue was raised earlier: actualizing individuals tend to obey inner directives despite any cry of outrage or criticism from without, from family, coworkers or friends.

A client of mine, one of the most integrated, talented young executives I've had the privilege to work with, serves as a good example in this regard. He recently decided to leave one corporation for another against the wishes of those he respects. In the first corporation, his path to a more senior position was blocked. Because he is chronologically younger than every other senior officer, he was expected to stay and patiently "wait his turn" for promotion. His leadership drives, giftedness and sense of destiny fueled his desire for a top spot in a major corporation. So he chose to leave. His colleagues and friends were shocked: they hadn't expected him to go; leaving was the harder course of action. He could have stayed put, earned a huge salary for five more years in what was (and still is) a prestigious national position, and then, after waiting his turn in properly "adjusted" fashion, would have been invited to take the top spot he wanted, probably before reaching his fortieth year. Staying would have been his safer, more acceptable option. No one thought he'd opt for the more challenging, riskier route.

He felt differently; felt pressed from within to move on. "This isn't even clear to me," he explained. "I have no concrete sense of what message I'm getting from myself. I do sense that I'm going to have several careers," he said, listing three diverse careers in general terms, and continued: "I know that people feel I should stay and wait. I might be thought impatient, maybe egotistical; anyone would be happy to wait, so what gives me the audacity to move on? I feel I must leave." His intuition about what's needed, his receptivity to interior cues are aptitudes that give that young man's decision making and choices such power and such good probability of succeeding.

However, this type of action, rooted as it is on illogical, unpopular "reasons" (i.e., unconscious stirrings and unclear, vague images), is what makes growth toward wholeness unpopular, so disliked. Even though here we see one man taking a shot at self-improvement, such efforts barely scratch the surface of the core self. As previous chapters indicated, wholeness is not an easy "business" assignment to tackle; being whole doesn't always look attractive to others. The mavericks, the aberrants, the maladapted (or nonconformists) are often those most likely to "sell all," risk everything, on behalf of their life's ideals. Unfortunately, such individuals do not always succeed—they get sidetracked, may feel ambivalent or be weakly motivated. Hence, the way of wholeness is less traveled.

Telling the truth about what we need, about insights and convictions takes courage and strength. Almost no one does all this completely, which may be the better part of wisdom. Who does even a bit of this truth telling without hesitation, struggle, resistance? When we voice who we really are and want, we risk going against everything the world (i.e., family, friends, community) holds dear. Raising our authentic voice also asks us to confront what we once thought was important but may no longer value. Often we are called "selfish." Worst of all, perhaps most frightening of all, we come up against our self-doubts about what we're doing, our fears about what we might do or might be giving up, or our past actions, desires to please others, to belong, have security. These needs are real in one sense. They can keep us stuck in untenable situations for years. Certainly such emotions can prevent us from hearing our innermost summons or protect us from gaining insights that might jeopardize a secure, well-adjusted life.

Yet it is clear that the actualizing psyche develops *only as* individuals discover and express what they're really about. That truthful expression is the cost and currency of wholeness. To do that, we must accept ourselves unconditionally. Moreover, there doesn't seem to be any one guide, course of study or experience so conductive to that growth as *time,* reflection, inner stillness and solitude. Spiritual direction or therapeutic dialogue may prove invaluable. To examine such elements and see how they promote the three major qualities of wholeness—authenticity, adaptability and intuition—I shall first address two rather generic abilities: patience and self-acceptance. Again, I term these "abilities" because they can be learned. These add much to a person's health, mental and physical, and not enough has been written about the value of these two abilities of wholeness.

The study participants are good guides in all this. We note, in reviewing their comments, that their subjective strength and stewardly, or transcendent, worldview came about gradually. In many cases people described a several year life-change. In some cases we heard comments like, "I knew it was something I had to do, even if it took the rest of my life." With the exception of the intense, rare conversion experience, such as Saint Paul's apparent encounter, it is likely that spiritual wholeness comes incrementally, over a period of years, not in a flash or as an "instantaneous" life-change. It is true that life changing insights happen in out-of-time instances. But insights must be digested, assimilated, translated into action to remedy some previous misperceptions, and decisions that grew out of these, to transform the quality and direction of life itself.

Time, therefore patience, is a critical, perhaps first, condition for self-development. Those whose sense of urgency or self-critical wish for instant "perfection" is such that they want to improve in a jiffy are probably suffering from such low self-esteem, such self-defeating expectations, that they are setting themselves up for failure. That failure then further intensifies the self-loathing that originally set up the urgency to be perfect. Such motives are usually stimulated by our idealized version of ourselves. In our fantasy we hold an unblemished image of ourselves; we believe we impress others with say, our superb power, intelligence or beauty. We need that image, much as we need to impress others, because, deep within, we feel impoverished, inadequate, powerless.

These mental pictures are self-defeating. Most of us are quite ordinary. By ordinary I don't mean commonplace. Rather I mean natural, unpretentious, genuine and complete in what we are and are not.

We cannot unfold wholeness through self-loathing, shame, a forced or rushed "program." Pressuring and brutalizing ourselves into self-improvement projects often aggravates and reinforces the very feelings of inadequacy and incompetence we're straining to get rid of. Indeed, we can only get "there" when we accept ourselves where we are, here and now. Improvements usually come when, subjectively, we let ourselves *be*. Just as a baby's teeth come in when ready and not when its parents want them to come in, we had best think of our growth as something completely natural that will occur in time, with nurturing, and once we get off our own backs. As American psychiatrist Fritz Kunkel once said, our problem is not to light the light. We're simply to remove the obstacles. Our only solution, it seems to me, is to get inwardly stronger and not cherish too idealized a picture of ourselves, of what we wish to be. To criticize and blame ourselves for what we are right now seems punitive and counterproductive.

Some techniques described in the next chapter may give us power and inner strength, thus increasing our ability to wait, to be patient and tolerate our flaws, like a mature parent who is raising a beloved child. Here, of course, we are examining spiritual growth of healthy adults—not methods to "cure" deep neurotics or, say, ax murderers.

Most growth techniques are demanding. They take time. They require regular practice. Developing patience is a first skill that we may wish to consider in our quest for wholeness. In other words, these techniques exact the very currency we need to pay. As we review the study participants' comments, we note their willingness to take that time. One participant described his inability to rid himself of a bad habit this way: "I've discovered that if I try to force myself into changing, the habit persists. It takes on a life of its own. If I can feel that I'm all right the way I am, that I really don't *have* to change in order to like myself, the habit begins to leave me. So I'm giving this thing another decade or so to work its way out of my being." This nonresisting, self-accepting attitude is not one most people can adopt. That may explain why so many fail who battle against their overindul-gences (e.g., overweight, alcohol consumption, smoking, etc.).

Our own vanity makes us imagine we can, in our human-ness, achieve a stainless perfection. The introvert, for example, who thinks he must be gregarious to be "perfect" is rejecting what he is in hope of being flawless. His best self will usually come to life as he accepts his tendency toward introversion, not by forc-ing some artificial social skill upon himself. If he can appreciate himself as reserved and reflective and let himself be (psychically speaking), chances are good that in this more relaxed state he will begin to enjoy others, will feel more like talking freely with them and might even enjoy socializing from time to time. Wholeness does not arrive by our willing it. Nor does it unfold through the use of some intellectualized formula. If anything, the reverse is true. By relaxing our grip on an inordinate need for perfection, we create a richer emotional atmosphere of acceptance and expe-rience a greater degree of integration.

We are healed to the extent that we love ourselves as we are right now: blemishes, vulnerabilities, warts and all. Not as we wish we were or will be at some time in some distant future. In other words, we cannot reject ourselves today and expect to accept ourselves someday. Only self-acceptance, love, can bring out wholeness. We gain that loving ability by practicing it on our-selves, and others, as we can *now*.

Of course, there is a catch-22 inherent in this, one that can only be resolved by "illogical" transcendent thinking. Because we must accept ourselves as we are now, while simultaneously hold-ing in mind the knowledge that we want to eliminate traits that impede our growth, that may be self-defeating or humiliating to us, we must move beyond the dilemma, rise above it. Intensive therapy could be required to lessen the self-hate separating us from our core self; self-hate and fear keep in place all the limita-tion, hopelessness and shame we experience. The only cure seems love: to accept ourselves even as we do things that we know, and feel, to be unacceptable.

I often suggest to clients that they adopt this mindset when observing them struggling in vain with some offensive flaw. The stance is first conceptual, a posture of unconditional love more than a technique. The inner stance goes something like this: "I've not yet rid myself of this habit (emotion, attitude, toxic relationship, addiction, etc.), but in time I'll outgrow it, much as I outgrew other limiting habits (traits, attitudes, emotions, etc.) in childhood. I'll be patient with myself, do everything I can to build self-respect, to choose that which inspires me and others, while trusting that in time I'll grow so things resolve themselves." Competent, trustworthy counseling at such points can also help tremendously.

If we can truthfully embrace ourselves in this way, which often involves little more than self-forgiveness for being imperfect, usually the problem or trait will disappear in time. The trick is to wholeheartedly mean it. This stance is not so different from the biblical edict in the New Testament that tells us to love the very one who is hard to love. Didn't Jesus continually teach that it didn't take any special goodness to do a man a good turn who has first done one for us? "And if you salute only your brethren, what more are you doing than others?" (Matt 5:47). To love our enemies must also mean we are to love ourselves, even when we are our own enemy. Yet such love, such generosity of heart, is inordinately hard to muster. This is why a trusting, ongoing dialogue with a spiritually intelligent helping professional is so often a wise choice.

Our Western culture's emphasis on instant cure-alls and self-perfection and flashy achievements makes that acceptance nearly impossible. One client, a powerfully successful entrepreneur, was grossly overweight. He was always in search of a miracle diet. When I suggested that his overeating might be a symptom of his own self-destruction, that the tendency might dissolve if he could accept himself as worthwhile, *even* as he saw himself fat, unable to control his eating, he replied that I was talking "moon language." He said that he couldn't stand to accept himself as fat. "If I accept myself as I am, I'll never change. I'll just keep on eating." To this day he is still gaining and losing and gaining weight.

There is a way out, a way to develop patience, self-acceptance and a more generous heart. Any number of solitary disciplines and practices, which our next chapter describes—even those we might combine with, say, "talk therapies"—are available to those who would be whole. These pave the way for intuition to develop and set the stage for a special kind of bonding-unto-self that precedes actualization and gives rest to the stressed and weary. These practices provide time-out to learn about ourselves, to build the fortitude and courage needed for the skills to reach what we know to be our highest spiritual good. Such practices may also structure into everyday life a contemplative solitude, silence and awareness. Without having to change anything, we can promote the kind of perceptual detachment needed for social and self-transcendence.

10
Solitude and Silence in the Development of Wholeness

At the end of my dialogue of prayer, I've developed a prayer motif:

> In my contingency and imperfectness, I need you,
> For your caring, I love you,
> For your sustaining, I trust you,
> For your holiness, I worship you,
> My Lord and My God.

I've discovered that the closeness which I crave, though not humanly present, is divinely right here all the time. My aloneness may be what I need to become dependent on and open toward God directly.

Participant, Alabama

Throughout the ages silence has been considered a way, a discipline, by which people could refine and deepen themselves. Most monastic orders take vows of silence whereby individuals direct all their physical and mental energies toward inner growth and God. Some churches—the Quakers, for example—fully value silence to this day and conduct their services largely in an atmosphere of silence.

In silence our reflective ability, and *need* to reflect, is nurtured. In silence we grow aware: we notice our hidden thoughts, our various fleeting emotions. In silence we perceive the ineffable, that which cannot be verbalized or made concrete. For those tending to wholeness, silence and solitude affirm individuality.

Sitting silently or speaking quietly within our own hearts and minds, we confront our past actions, aspirations, our most cherished dreams. Not only do we meet ourselves in silence, but the silence heals us as well. Here, in the still, immovable, changeless core self, we can find safety to face pain, and ultimately find safety to meet our most sacred, essential self. Thus we rediscover and renew ourselves, at the heart.

Something in us—energy, life-source, our positive will to live—is strengthened by silence, much as our physical bodies are strengthened by sleep. It is not just the absence of sounds but the *presence* of a positive, complete world in itself—a world in which it is permissible, even desirable, to see ourselves, accept ourselves, as we really are. The Swiss philosopher Max Picard proposes other benefits to silence:

> Where silence is, man is observed by silence. Silence looks at man more than man looks at silence. Man does not put silence to the test.[1]

Silence can be our Yoga, one form of self-discipline. We look more closely at a variety of forms of Yoga shortly. At this point, we note that Swami Paramananda, one of the first Hindu spiritual teachers to influence American thought, taught that silence had the power to cultivate patience:

> The deep things do not come suddenly. Let us be patient—with ourselves. We may recognize many defects in our natures…it can all be removed. Go on working silently.
> Silence and patience go together. Silence has wonderful creative power. Make a study of the lives of great men. They conceive an idea but they do not go out and shout it before the world; they think silently and work quietly until they realize their ideal.[2]

While many of us find it nearly impossible to arrange life in ways that mirror the study participants, almost anyone who really wants to can carve out a time and place each day in which to sit quietly, perhaps with eyes closed. Or, as a friend does, to just relegate a portion of each evening to silence, where no telephones, television or radio interrupt. It is in silence that my friend takes her evening meal, and in silence spends an entire afternoon each Sunday. She has found these periods organize and center her life and that she gains much energy for new ideas and projects. For those who say they are too busy to add such a discipline, my opinion is that they *are* too busy. They may be resisting their own growth.

It can be impractical to move to the woods or leave a secure job, family or friends. And that relocation could be unnecessary. What is necessary, and highly practical, is to create simple routines and structure in our lives so that we can meditate, reflect, sit in quiet and thus grow in understanding.

Any number of solitary practices assist in developing wholeness. By solitary practices I mean various formal meditations such as the ancient forms of prayer common to our Judeo-Christian mystical traditions. And practices such as the Zen procedure called *zazen* or classical mantra meditations that originated in India before Christ, can now be learned in the West through such large organizations as the Transcendental Meditation movement or smaller, more personal instruction such as found in the Kirpal Light Satsang.

Even some physical disciplines, for instance the Eastern martial arts (e.g., Aikido, to name one form) or long-distance running, fit the category of disciplines I am describing. Because meditation is such an intimate choice, it is not my aim to recommend any one activity over another, even though serious students of one discipline may be highly critical of some procedures, while strongly recommending others. This discussion hopes to encourage readers to examine the benefits of any reliable, traditional form of meditation, then responsibly investigate which specific practice might provide the greatest advantages for their individual needs.

It may seem abrupt for us to jump from a description of the study participants' lives to discussing meditative techniques (especially in view of the fact that the study participants didn't dwell on meditation or physical disciplines), but upon closer inspection the shift makes sense.

We have read that the study participants know the importance of "time out." They all spoke of the desire to have quality "free" time. Many live alone by choice. In this way they can spend a great deal of time silently. Those who are married have described various strategies for structuring solitude, privacy and silence into their lives. Somehow, in stillness and in the wholly sequestered space of their inner life, they were able to identify what they valued and needed, and arrange their lives to provide that. I suggest meditation, even simple sitting in silence, can order our thinking so that answers we crave for living more intelligently will surface. When one's whole existence is arranged simply, as illustrated by so many of the study participants, distractions and encumbrances dissolve. With time to pray, reflect, read, walk about in the beauty of nature, life reflects a natural ebb and flow, becoming much like a meditation. In the words of one individual, "I don't meditate per se, but then my whole life is so balanced that I'm in a contemplative state all the time." Another said, "I've become so aware of the micro/macro phenomenon all around me that my awareness is always open. I sit at my table, observe the colors of the trees or listen to the birds, the movement of the leaves, and I am transfixed. It's as if I'm keenly awake during all activity. I've done a lot of Yoga in the past, and feel that now my entire life is a Yoga of sorts. I'm *in* every act, in each moment, in a way that supplies a radiant sort of energy for me."

We can achieve these benefits, that same inner posture, by setting aside part of each day for a period of silence and solitude. Selected meditative and solitary practices help develop psychic health because the stillpoint of being, our innermost core, can, at first, only be reached indirectly: through understanding dreams, through flashes of insight, feelings and symbols, and all this by stilling the mind. These paragraphs suggest that almost anyone regardless of age or economic circumstances can move toward wholeness in an independent, private manner by creating some simple lifestyle adjustments and, after judicious research, adopting a contemplative discipline. Some people should not practice such disciplines without expert guidance, perhaps even medical advice.

According to psychiatrist William Glasser, a discipline must meet six requirements if it is to help us grow healthier. It should be...

- noncompetitive and be done, for the most part, alone.

- a practice that is independent of others for its execution.

- easy to do; should not require much mental effort (e.g., straining to make the mind blank turns people away from meditation despite their sound intentions).

- a practice that is done regularly, about one hour per day (or twice a day in equal amounts of time).

- something that the doer *believes* will improve his or her mental/physical state. We must see our improvements without needing an "expert" or guru to tell us we're getting better; in other words, in every respect, it should build self-sufficiency rather than dependence upon another.

- something that can be done without inordinate self-criticism or comparison to someone else's progress. We hurt ourselves and our developmental progress when we think, "I'm not running as far, fast or gracefully as John," or when we cruelly ridicule ourselves for the form or manner in which we see ourselves performing our practice.[3]

The sum total of accumulated meditative experiences ought to be such that we discover our strengths and weaknesses and come to terms with ourselves nonjudgmentally. We have already seen that self-acceptance and patience are necessary corollaries to positive growth; as we proceed it may be clearer why such disciplines are so helpful in developing these qualities. A contemplative discipline seems critical to any discussion of social or self-transcendence. These two values are, in the final analysis, a coming-to-terms with the self in an honest, accepting, self-trusting way.

As one begins a discipline, it is natural to wonder if an expert, a training course or "master" are needed. Fortunately, little formal instruction is necessary, although some believe that spiritual direction or competent therapeutic guidance may smooth the way, and that the initiation process is also highly instrumental in obtaining productive results. Others feel there is much to be gained through the relationship with a master. The Bible of course makes many references to meditation, and ancient Eastern and classical Judeo-Christian mystical-meditative practices became traditions without extensive, expensive, weekend seminars. Consider the psalmists who prayed intently, one imagines prompted only by God. Rigorous discipline, however, on the part of the meditator, and belief in the value of the practice have always been essential.

To answer, "Why do such disciplines promote the growth to unitive health?" it may help to juxtapose the characteristics and functional aspects of wholeness against the impact that selected meditative practices have upon subjective health.

Self-realized individuals know themselves in the Socratic sense. This implies truthfulness to self and others, even when that truth may carry with it the cost of inconvenience, rejection or even physical danger. It also means that they know themselves at their "best": recovering a relationship with their integrity, previously sacrificed and discarded uniqueness, their sacred interiority is complete and lacking nothing. This is why, in our previous chapters on the mystic type, we heard evidence in the words of some participants of people who wanted nothing. They delighted in the simplest things, as if they had everything they could possibly want. Their satiety gives us a clue to the integration that exists in the actualizing individual: he or she has resolved many dichotomies of life, reconciled many conflicts, and is living in "Being-cognition"—in the awareness of creative or spiritual intelligence, the highest Self. This satisfied state must not be mistaken for a "why-try?" humdrum lethargy. Nothing could be further from the truth.

The interpersonal and transpersonal worlds of completed, or actualizing, individuals are integrated. As such, these individuals move spontaneously from within to without, responding to inner promptings, values and aspirations. In moment-to-moment living, they move in awe or wonderment, their consciousness saturated with a sense of richness, surplus, superordinate affluence.

In relationship to others, they may be highly discriminating, preferring their own company or the company of family and a few close friends to an endless yet superficial stream of associations with people they can only know slightly. On the other hand, they may move easily in social situations, sincerely enjoying everyone. In either case, one is not simply passive, not just an amused or blissfully detached observer of others and one's own interior life.

From insights flow actions. Actualizing individuals are in the process of becoming more purposeful, more vigorous in the areas of their interests. In all other areas they may be run-of-the-mill. In the domain of their particular inclinations or talents, they will often show passionate involvements. Be these parents, craftspersons, thinkers or artists, at the very least they are absorbed with, and propelled by, their own internal images and values. They *choose*—and this is a key competency—to turn their intrapsychic world into life-activity and realistic, that is, workable, outcomes. This translation makes such individuals seem unique. In fact, they are unique; are tapping into a special, unknown reality, a one-of-a-kind world—their own inner cosmos. From that is shaped something tangible, contributive, for self-and-others. Maslow used the phrase "SA creativeness" to mean that the self-actualizing exhibited a tendency to do *anything* creatively: cooking, homemaking, teaching, building a business, speaking, etcetera. He contrasted S/A creativity with that which springs from inborn talent, such as artistic or poetic gifts.

The tendency of S/A creatives to spontaneously self-express without inordinate fear or self-strangulation is also one by-product of individuals made more spiritually potent when propelled by the added energy, certainty and life-direction derived from contemplative practices. It seems essential to repeat that there are degrees of actualization, that what I am primarily addressing throughout these pages, and more closely in this chapter, is a progression by which we experience lessened fear, a changed mind and heart, an alteration of energy and will in the direction of that which is healthier,—more positive, more loving, mature, responsible, independent and life-promoting.

These shifts gradually prompt an altered self and worldview. They also bring about an enhanced, more committed relationship with self and others because we gain strength to stick with our project and goals, gain courage to be truthful, gain ability to really love the other as self.

I am talking about simple subjective health, completion of an interior sort: what each of us would be (in fact, longs to be) were we whole. Actualization is our most natural state. This is the issue that gives one such trouble with the mentality of many psychologists, psychiatrists, social workers, etcetera. Instead of guiding us out of our misery or waking us up to what we could be, many helping professionals sustain our neurotic, separated condition by encouraging us to adjust bravely to the world. The world should, for the most part, be helped to adjust to *us* since, as has been said, *the world is made for us—we are not made for it.* The psychiatric tradition still seems to treat actualization as an oddity, a rare event. Yet, as noted, to be actualizing is a human being's most natural state. If only we had the proper guidance and information, most could grow in that direction. Sadly, it's usual for us to miss the mark of our potential since we're so eager to adjust to society's conditions of "normalcy."

Were "average" persons to take time to turn inward, to develop themselves in the ways of wholeness, their behavior, choices, activities could tend to become intrinsically motivated. Each act and choice could have more meaning and fluidity. Such authentic actions are the result of a conversion process that can be experienced whether we are grocery clerks, grade school dropouts, nuclear scientists or "bums." This progression, happily, is the great equalizer that, being spiritual, has little to do with social standing.

In this study we have continually seen that the participants pare down life—remove many distractions from their daily doings so that they can have the time and the climate to commune honestly with themselves and others for a more meaningful life. One suspects the desire to lead a simplified life comes only *after* the self-forgetting, transcending, integrating phenomenon has begun: that, say, "voluntary simplicity" is a result of an emerging wholeness.

No one really knows "why" some people are blessed with the tendency toward actualization while others continue to reject their best selves. The key to subjective adult health may be found in childhood. It is here that the primary trust relationship with self develops and takes on its positive or negative tone.

Researcher Maya Pines's study of children whom she called "invulnerables" holds special interest for us now. In her article, "Superkids,"[4] Pines explored the reasons for the superior life-success of about 15 percent of those who had had horrendous early life experiences. Something in these children's traumatic early lives seemed to strengthen, rather than thwart, their development.

They not only survived, they flourished into competent, capable adults. Their autonomy, adaptability and intuitive brightness developed while they were still young.

As adults, they showed themselves to be independent thinkers, yet retained strong interpersonal skill. Many of the 15 percent became community leaders. As inordinately skilled adaptors, these children could offer us clues about how optimal human development occurs.

The traits Pines described as being helpful to adult functioning were most evident in the children of schizophrenics who had to protect themselves from their parents' illness. To survive their early environments, they developed strategic self-defenses that then served them the rest of their lives. In the midst of physical and emotional trauma, these capable children managed to withdraw successfully into themselves and were also able to locate at least one healthy adult figure with whom to relate. In solitude and separateness, they sorted out and ordered their chaotic world into some sensible whole. They drew from their chaos a lasting, sustaining inner strength. From their relationship with one healthy adult they learned to relate to others. In some intuitive, mysterious way that contradicts a social scientist's logic they managed to grow up intact, without either turning their backs on themselves or being split in half. Is this grace?

Their growing up involved a long, lonely struggle against odds most other children do not survive. Their sense of being unique, different and alone may have provided them with just the right foundation for the independent, intuitive thinking and autonomous behavior needed to protect their sanity and enable them to fend for themselves.

It is precisely the lonely task of ordering their disruptive lives and coming to terms with feelings of alienation or separateness that allows people to develop such lasting self-trust, a firm sense of who they are and what they could and need to do in life. I suggest that the solitary sorting-out process is also what adults *must* do to increase their own interior health.

The normal adjustment of the average man or woman implies a buying into the established worldview, with all that suggests, at the expense of true potential. Most children, for example, willingly trade their own insights, feelings and aspirations for those of their parents. In the process, they grow up slavishly bartering their joy, freedom, ability to love for approval or security. As noted, even consulting a psychiatrist when the individual feels stuck, feels dishonest or impotent is no guarantee of release, as R. D. Laing writes in his *The Divided Self*:

> Psychiatry could be, and some psychiatrists are, on the side of transcendence, of genuine freedom, and of true human growth. But psychiatry can so easily be a technique of brainwashing, of inducing behavior that is adjusted....Thus I would wish to emphasize that our "normal" "adjusted" state is too often the abdication of ecstasy, the betrayal of our true potentialities, that many of us are only too successful in acquiring a false self to adapt to false realities.[5]

The other ingredient necessary to emotional health, which Pines's research subjects possessed, is the ability to see oneself as competent, able to stick with difficulty even when, subjectively, it feels natural to quit.

Pines's writings did not phrase it this way, but these children became socially transcendent in much the same way the adults in my study do: *they consciously chose to step back from their environment, to observe and manage it with detachment.*[6] Although in Pines's group the detachment and withdrawal process seems to have happened at an earlier age, in both our studies detachment seems most often to occur because of survival needs: the individual feels, as one man put it, "I had to back out of my situation emotionally; it was a question of life or death: *my* life or *my* death, however gradual. I knew I simply could not continue to exist in the situation as it was."

Harvard professor Abraham Zaleznik describes an additional cluster of traits developed by those who manage to pull back into themselves, to establish an interior rapport. In his article "Managers and Leaders, Are They Different?"[7] he describes leaders who sound much like Pines's superkids, saying that their lives are marked by a sense of being different; they continually struggle to sort out, order and make the world in which they live comprehensible.

From their earliest days, born leaders question things. They are often alienated, experience a "profound separateness" and seem to be people who sort out life's questions alone. They also face rather than avoid their difficulties, as did study participants who spoke of facing their dark times and conflicts alone. These proclivities reward Zaleznik's leaders with their "tough bite on life." I suggest that such traits are also essential to actualizing individuals.

Although Pines and Zaleznik were portraying unusually competent children and leaders respectively, the characteristics of these two groups match the characteristics of well-integrated people. As with those in Pines's and Zaleznik's studies, actualizing adults initiate their own development through a reflective process. This may be painful at the start, but later benefits them and eventually benefits others. These individuals ultimately relate to self-and-others as whole, whereas previously they related as alienated or separate.

Self-reliance and subjective fortitude are benefits of their reflective protocols. At the core of their feelings of strength we find self-trust, self-respect. Having no one else to lean on, or choosing not to lean on anyone else, these individuals begin to lean on themselves. Thus they learn to trust their self-governance.

Author Joseph Chilton Pearce writes that, while in infancy, our mind develops a bond (he defines this as forms of rapport and communication) with a "primary matrix." The primary matrix, as we might guess, is the mother.

Matrix, according to Pearce, is derived from the Latin "womb." From this word we get the words *matter, material*, and *mother.* Out of these conceptual frames come the physical forms of life. Eventually, our mind shifts its mother-as-matrix feelings to the world. As patiently we think, read, study, perhaps engage in healing—therapeutic or spiritual—dialogue, an interior move to wholeness takes root. With that the false self, with its fears and programmed reactions, loses hold in awareness.

When we as children feel safe in the primary matrix (i.e., safe within the subjective/actual experience of our mother), we eventually believe that the world, our new matrix of the larger environment, is a safe place too.

I agree with Pearce that few children form the kind of secure bond that children were meant to have. In the case of Pines's group called "invulnerables," *these children learned to fend for themselves so well because they actually recreated their matrix for themselves; in a way, they were their own mothers,*[8] ultimately learning to trust the self-matrix, of course, as a bond-to-self. The self-matrix was, for them, safe, and so led to their feeling safe in the world. Because they related so successfully from inner to outer worlds, because, as children, they discovered that they could capably handle the world of others as well as circumstances, in their adult life they possessed enhanced competency.

Many people do not undertake this arduous homework of building inner strength, as noted. Perhaps many don't need to. Others seem separated from their highest self, live contracted, emotionally stunted lives. Thus a distrusting core of feelings about self-as-matrix follow into adulthood. When we distrust ourselves or we feel that there are a host of unpredictable circumstances to face and that other people are unknowable or threatening, then we distrust our world. We feel ill prepared to strike out on our own. Strictly speaking, the average person is closed off and guarded, cut off from the core self, his or her most capable, tender, creative self. To know *this* self we must tap our inner depths and be open to primary thought processes and inward directives.

We have seen that rich rewards come to those who reframe, reinterpret and recreate their paradigm of self-and-other. When the necessary work of bonding to self has been completed (and now I am referring to the highest self: the one mystics and theologians label "Self"), the regeneration of a new, trustworthy, even friendly matrix takes place. Individuals who feel subjectively safe are emotionally connected and experience no separation, splitting or fragmentation. We don't *feel* isolated or alone because, in a realistic fashion, we are bonded, safe, "at-one-with." Maharishi Mahesh Yogi calls this feeling "Mother is at home," and probably every emotionally healthy individual has had that subjective sense.

The interior work of establishing self-trust, meaning and order develops character traits (or aptitudes, as I've called these earlier) that we ultimately link with actualization. This has a chicken-or-egg feel to it: are people who tackle their inner homework of ordering chaos and reconciling naturally inclined to solitary, silent introspection? Or are their early lives indeed so oppressive that eventually, whether in childhood or later, they must think through their problems independently or disintegrate?

I'm reminded here of the study participant who said that, for him, the sense of separation was "insanity." Apparently, his "world-as-matrix" was so chaotic and dangerous that he had to sort things out or suffer dire consequences. This suggests that there are degrees to feelings of separation: for one it means insanity; for another mild anxiety; and for yet another, just a "normal" state to become accustomed to, with its constant tensions.

Whatever the degree, whatever our reasons for initially detaching, or walking an inward path, the lengthy, solitary, ordering progression—effectively undertaken—builds. This culminates, when done healthfully, in the individual's establishing a secure foundation for thinking and acting independently. This means we can become heavily, if not totally, self-referring. Also, by trusting our actions and directions, we become someone others also can trust. At that point, we ourselves are perceived to be predictable, all of a piece, understandable, knowable. Anyone like that is sensed to provide sending constant, consistent messages rather than sending mixed signals.

From both a professional and individual standpoint, I now sense that most adults can build a secure framework with which to live if—and it is a big if—they are willing to plunge into the work of inner regeneration: the pulling away, self-scrutiny and self-acceptance/self-trust steps outlined. These steps involve questioning our previous life-decisions: how we have "adjusted," what attitudes we have formed to face everyday situations, relationships, our life's work, the beliefs with which we face everyday tasks and so on. If we fear our thoughts, need others too much, are overly self-critical or severely attached to our belief systems, we may not be ready for such work.

The challenge includes changing our minds about almost everything. To establish a bond with ourselves, with an unseen yet essential part of ourselves, may mean questioning how we've learned to view the world. If we view it as unfriendly, for example, or wonder why everyone doesn't feel this way, this might be a good place to start. If we feel that, say, joy, love or doing work we enjoy are not meant for us, that might pinpoint areas to probe. Why do we feel left out of love or provision? Where did we learn our rules? Who taught us our values and expectations? How happy were the people who told us the world was this way or that? How fulfilled were our teachers? How much joy and love did *they* express and experience?

If we are willing to take on the job we will have to question our decisions and beliefs. Taking such issues to heart offers enormous advantages: those who trust themselves in a deeply constant fashion develop a subjective sense of safety and confidence. There is transparency here. They will waste little time surveying others for their opinions or defending themselves against their own desires, aspirations and feelings. They are able to focus on meaningful work, goals, friendships. We are not describing perfection—just that these individuals "possess" more of themselves to utilize for enjoyment, for spontaneous relationship, creative expression, playing, for fruitful living as they desire.

Here is an ironic twist: we as individuals must trust an unknown, invisible, creative part of ourselves as a condition of wholeness; we must be willing to face what heretofore we may have feared—our own shadow, our demons and cowardly, perhaps loathed, secret self that we might have rejected, hidden, often successfully. There is ample resistance and natural reluctance to start this work, a resistance almost everyone shares. So comes faith.

Many of us deny ourselves the opportunity of knowing and drawing out something more from within. Out of fear, lethargy (usually resistance in disguise) or indecision, we believe that such inner work is foolish, that people don't change, that change is impossible or dangerous, at least for us. Wholeness, on the other hand, demands we energize ourselves, if only in imagination, strengthen ourselves from within in some ways we have avoided.

In my corporate practice, when I sense that an individual yearns for wholeness and is willing to do the requisite inner work, I often recommend that he or she start meditating, and/or see a therapist and/or perhaps take up a physical discipline that fits the conditions specified earlier. All that starts by taking full responsibility for researching, as well as beginning, the specific therapy or discipline.

Effectual meditation appears to regenerate and reconstruct the psyche. In some ways it is similar to the psychotherapeutic process: it introduces meditators to a deeper self that they may have been avoiding. At the very least, regular meditation alleviates certain physical stresses, enabling one to feel more gratified, safer, less anxious, less despairing. In its ultimate form, a meditation program may enable us to reap the fruits of our fullest humanity, whether we call this enlightenment, actualization, Being, or Selfhood. Since there are various types and schools of meditation, we have to select wisely in order to gain the ultimate benefit. Those who pray, meditate, study sacred literature and engage in competently run counseling seem to have an ideal mix for spiritual growth.

When, through an effective meditation procedure, we free our hidden, creative self, we meet our authentic, intuitive nature. Perhaps we gradually accept in ourself that which we have rejected, that which has made us seem unlike others. Most classical forms of meditation, whether familiar Western forms of prayer or chanting, or seemingly esoteric Eastern disciplines, bring into awareness previously unconscious bits of experience, eventually allowing us to assimilate these into a unified whole, or *gestalt*.

Jung wrote that the hidden self was like a shadow, that without the shadow we are only half of ourselves. Many decades later, Fritz Perls, called the father of Gestalt psychology, reinforced this notion, stressing the importance of *assimilation* to human development.

By assimilation, Perls meant taking in and absorbing (through active and conscious awareness) bits of repressed memories and past experiences that, in the unassimilated state, fragment, drain and weaken psychic health. He likened the assimilation process to chewing up food; undigested morsels will return, unpleasantly, to cause trouble for us. To Perls, unacknowledged emotions and experiences sap energy, sowing seeds for conflict and neurosis: "The awareness of, and the ability to endure, unwanted emotions are the *conditio sine qua non* for a successful...cure. This process (i.e., assimilation) forms the *via regia* to health."⁹

Meditation offers an opportunity to become aware of, endure and ultimately assimilate unwanted emotions so that they fade into the background. Emotions become understandable in the context of our entire life, endurable through our meditative experience; we see ourselves, feel ourselves, *watch* ourselves enduring these conditions. It is a reliving and a proper digestion of buried "content."

One reason hypnosis, visualization and other types of suggestion or trancelike processes may not be as efficacious is because in these practices we strive to attain something (even if only a relaxed state of mind). In striving, "doing," we often direct the attention rather than simply observing or dwelling on what is. In meditation, we become consciously aware of whatever passes through the mind; thus our attention "watches" thought impartially, as a by-product of the act of "dwelling." This could sound nonsensical to the nonmeditator who lacks experience of pure awareness that comes with meditation, but there it is.

All meditation involves a dwelling upon something: a word, a flame, a mantra, a phrase, a breath. Our mind occupied in this way, brings the attention to deeper, more subtle levels of being, eventually transcending thought so that the mind becomes pure awareness. The meditator develops an inner posture that (like a spotlight on the attention) shines itself on an ever larger screen of thoughts and images—both in and out of meditation. While meditating, effectual meditators gain a front-row seat as witnesses to their mental phenomenon, thus gaining objectivity over thoughts and fleeting images, since anything that can be observed objectively can be controlled.

Rather than remaining trapped experiencers to our emotions, as meditators we are gradually liberated, able to endure emotionally what, in ordinary consciousness, we felt unendurable. What we previously avoided, suppressed or buried surfaces in awareness. As meditators we go through an inner alchemy, much like Pines's superkids, Zaleznik's developing leaders or our study participants in the earliest stages of actualizing. Like these others, now we face, sort out, organize and utilize conflicts, resistances and inner bits of experience, assimilating these for growth, while developing strength and self-trust.

Observing whatever we have suppressed could be enormously rewarding. Shying away from emotions drains creative potential, saps energy. Repressing and pretending things are not what they are weakens character. However, more than simply allowing us to squarely face unpleasantries, by meditating we develop in yet another major way. These solitary disciplines appear to cultivate an inner quality that Dr. Claude Naranjo and Professor Robert Ornstein call a "modality of being:"

> This presence or mode of being transforms whatever it touches…it might be said that the attitude or inner posture of the meditator is both his path and his goal.

For the subtle, invisible how is not merely a how to meditate, but a how to be....

The practice of meditation can be better understood as a...persistent effort to detect and become free from all conditioning, compulsive functioning of mind and body, habitual emotional responses that may contaminate the utterly simple situation required by the participant.[10]

Meditation seems capable of lowering stress and enhancing health. It creates a simple, silent inner witness and an ethical, accepting stance. I said earlier that it may not be necessary to withdraw physically from society or actually change a lifestyle in order to grow whole. Social and self-transcendence can be cultivated by those seriously willing to undertake the self-discipline of a daily meditation routine and perhaps, for some, also ongoing therapeutic counseling. Thus we can structure into life a silence, a keener self-awareness, a spiritual obedience (i.e., to the higher Self), inviting an inner transformation of the sort and quality described throughout this book.

There are so many forms of meditation that it is impossible to list them all in a brief comparative manner here. Many *physical* disciplines (Yoga, walking) are more appealing to some of us than prayer, working on a journal, or outside spiritual readings. Some types of devotional visualization or mindful walking might also center the attention on the never-ending action and antics of the restless mind. Only a few forms of rigorous meditation serve the conversion process under examination. In my opinion, traditional contemplative practices draw one deeply into inner silence, promote a level of transcendence not available to us in the ordinary waking state. Through this, our human nature touches the center of our spiritual ground of being, eventually releasing our "higher" nature.

Those who are mystically inclined are usually spontaneously drawn to such practices and tend to develop an intimate
fellowship with that in them which is most sacred. In *Finding
Grace at the Center,* we read of a traditional Christian prayer called
centering prayer, a classical form of meditation:

> By turning off the ordinary flow of thoughts, which
> reinforces one's habitual way of looking at the world,
> one's world begins to change…if you turn off your
> ordinary thought patterns, you enter into a new world
> of reality. To do this systematically, take up a position
> that will enable you to sit still. Close your eyes….
> Then slow down the normal flow of thoughts by
> thinking just one thought. Choose a sacred word of
> one or two syllables that you feel comfortable with. A
> one-syllable word such as God or Love is best.[11]

Such instructions propose that, as we continue, we enter a
deeper state of reality. This marks a beginning, not an end point,
of development; this state of reality can be our healer, not anything or anyone external. We undertake our centering prayer by
"dying" to self (the small egoistic self) and by dedication to God.
This way of devotion tends to "open" the heart, allowing the tender emotions and values of the spirit to grow.

As actualizing individuals attain a renewed awareness and a
steady bond with the inner self, they begin to be established in
subjective security. This may amount to a Taoistic "let be" or in
the Judeo-Christian framework a "God's will be done." In essence,
that is not so much experiencing a futile helplessness of outer
conditions as it is faithfully knowing things will work out, will
resolve because at one's ground of being, they *are* already
resolved. Nonresistance, such as this sense reveals, is a key to
"solving" all things, a form of faithful acceptance, and an active
choice to love.

Prayer, meditation and contemplation do more than calm the mind or open the heart. These steady the body. Many physicians now prescribe meditation and/or regular, noncompetitive exercise (like brisk walking, Yoga, jogging or swimming) for patients suffering from hypertension, or over-reactive nervous systems or even digestive problems. There is no neat mind/body split. What helps our mind gain rest from constant seeking, grasping, worrying, also helps the body. Growing numbers of researchers document the physiological benefits of meditation.

Dr. William Glasser's study of long-term runners and meditators suggest these physical benefits are woven in with psychological ones. His research indicates that a mix of blessings comes to those who are, in his words, "positively addicted" to their disciplines. To paraphrase his findings, over time, these people developed:

- subjective feelings of inner confidence, self-trust, outward serenity, calm or grace;
- creative thinking aptitudes;
- the ability to resolve inner conflicts and/or expanded ability to spot new or varied options in problem solving;
- a firmer sense of self, including the willingness to speak up and take action on behalf of what they sense is right and true for them;
- an increased ability to cope with pressure, manage stress and deal with ambiguity and change.[12]

By reviewing the traits of actualizing we quickly see these traits and Glasser's aptitudes are one and the same.

Almost any classic practice may further spiritual growth, provided it fits the criteria listed. I am wary of most commercial meditation programs, with the possible exceptions of the Zen Buddhist movement, the TM program and some less well-known but seemingly spotless teachings. Although dissimilar, these procedures instruct individuals in rather ancient forms of meditation, leaving them free to do the program on their own, without the trappings of ashrams, dogma or psychosocial political nuances. There must be many organized schools that do not require us to abandon our own religious heritage, while strengthening us in whatever heritage we do have. I am loathe to recommend programs that entice one to adopt their way of life as a condition of affiliation. Such enticements seem the very essence of enculturation, or social programming, that actualization avoids and seeks to overcome.

Ram Dass tells a story that sums this up: God and Satan were walking along the street together when God bent down and picked something up. Curious, as always, Satan inquired of the Lord, "What is that you have there?" As the Lord gazed at the thing, glowing brightly in his hand, he replied, "This is Truth." Whereupon Satan reached out for it, saying as he grasped at it, "Here, let me have it. I'll organize it for you."

Individuals who grow whole learn to think for themselves. They become self-referring, rather than other- or world-referring: progressively they design life from an intra-psyche perspective rather than from rules, idols and status symbols of society. Simply substituting one cultural overlay of beliefs and expectations for another will not do. Nothing short of full authenticity is required. That, as we have seen, involves steadfast loyalty to the demands of the inner kingdom. As difficult as this seems, perhaps nothing involves more struggle than accepting ourselves for what we are, warts and all. Even the most integrated of individuals have proclivities they would change if they could. This wish, too, must be given up if we wish to grow whole. Author Andre Gide once said that what seems different in ourselves is the rare thing we each possess, the one thing that gives us our worth. That's just what we try to suppress. Yet we claim to love life!

For such self-acceptance perhaps nothing (except meditation, prayer and the occasional session of, say, spiritual direction) surpasses the use of the spiritual diary. In the journal procedure we track inner growth, dreams, ideas and establish a dialogue with ourselves on a regular, systematic basis. Recently, through the writings of Kirpal Singh, I have come across a model of a spiritual diary with potential. For one thing, one can track daily life from the vantage point of unique qualities. For another, spiritual types can use the diary as a way of remembering God. Also, the diary serves as a vehicle for confessing one's failings. If we're the only ones who will read comments, at least we remain honest with ourself, as Kirpal Singh writes:

> Let your confessions be honestly and openly recorded in the various columns, so that you know where you stand and can take rectifying action. The best and easiest way to cure your ills is to yearn to be free of them....Once you become aware of a failure, you should be able to trace it to a certain situation, and this situation will help you to identify the cause of the weakness in you that has to be strengthened. By and by, the very cause of the failure will drop off by itself.[13]

The first mark of self-acceptance is willingness to *look* at ourselves honestly. Thus the logic for contemplative exercises and journal writing. The next step is having the humility to acknowledge that we are imperfect, that for us to be happy the world need not circle around us or bow to us as demigods. Only narcissism, the egocentric self, demands flawless perfection. This it interprets as that artificial sameness matching the world's idea of "perfect." Perfect, in a spiritual sense, can also mean spiritually complete, needing nothing, having within all that is needed. This is what Jesus Christ spoke about when he said, "Be perfect, therefore, even as your heavenly Father is perfect" (Matt 5:48).

To gain this type of completion we must give ourselves the *time* in which to grow. Wholeness does not come overnight. True, insights come in a flash, in a burst of out-of-time experience, but it may take years to translate insights into behavior. We make haste slowly, as the old adage advises: to embody what we realize is true, we may need to organize our life so as to offer options to grow in edifying choices and habits. That means being patient and designing life with an eye toward gaining reflective time. We need more than our weekends, more than just a Sunday retreat, to devote our entire life to a progression that has no limit or end to its wholesome growth.

Hence, our next commitment is to discipline ourselves sufficiently for the unstructured or contemplative time we need. That could mean saying no to social distractions or evenings spent with the television. It could mean saying no to family and friends who expect us to spend time in other or meaningless ways. Again, here's when we may need a counselor to help us grapple with the relational aspects of spiritual growth. Strong resentments could crop up when one family member (say, a spouse) wishes to pursue meditation or journal keeping, while another expects life to continue as it always has.

Seeking out competent help along the way may not be necessary: that all depends on where we are emotionally, what our circumstances are and how we choose to see or meet the situation. Also, our needs at one point in growth will not be those of another. Our trusted helpers may change. One wise counselor told me, years ago, that as growth is a lifelong process, the counselors and teachers we need for our unfolding are certain to change: "Don't be too proud to seek assistance. Two-way dialogue is only practical," he said. "And don't be too reluctant to let go when that time comes. You may need to move on for a while alone, and then another teacher will appear. All are useful if you assume responsibility for choosing them, for working with them, and for letting go when it is time."

Fritz Kunkel suggested it is also helpful to examine the biographies of people who reflect "well-lived" lives to learn how they overcame problems and elevated themselves. He stressed it was not necessary to read about *famous* people, because within the lives of ordinary people we find illustrations of creative ways of dealing with obstacles and opportunities for growth.

Above all, we must not seek out growth through harsh or artificial use of gimmicky techniques that we adopt, hoping to hype ourselves into wholeness. Neither does authenticity come when self-talk is negative, shame- or guilt-producing, or if we subject ourselves to endless harangues about what we "should" be doing, thinking, feeling. Happy are we who do not condemn ourselves.

It does not take inordinate material wealth or superhuman will to live creatively. All that is needed is that we design life to express those values that are most meaningful and elegant, most life sustaining. And we need not always look to others as role models or reassurers. After a certain point we may need to relinquish outside authority and focus on our own resolve and resourcefulness.

What we seek, seeks us. The goal of life is life—whatever we call it, with us, life ever present as our very breath. We will recognize, at first through faith, that within lives a profound, unseen power pervading existence that heals, guides, inspires. The design or redesign of our way of life is secondary; that is why there are as many "forms" of lifestyle as people. Our primary task is to understand what is, for us, most authentic. If, on the other hand, we try to adjust ourselves too closely, mechanistically, to that which experts, gurus or trends tell us is right and good or even required, we may sacrifice our fuller experience for something less than we deserve.

Almost anyone willing to undertake the regenerative work of getting in touch with him- or herself can experience both social and self-transcendence, although the latter seems, to me, a grace. And these values may be the wellsprings out of which clarified thinking, motives and acting flow. For these put us in touch with ourselves as we essentially are, instead of as we may sometimes feel. In this way, we come to know and to be our most wholesome, generous self: our highest Self.

Notes

Introduction

1. Marsha Sinetar, "Management in the New Age," *Personnel Journal* (September 1980): p. 749–55.

1. Advancement to Wholeness

1. Dorothy B. Phillips, ed., *The Choice Is Always Ours* (Illinois: Theosophical Publishing House, 1975), p. 45.

2. Paul Tillich, *The Courage To Be* (New Haven: Yale University Press, 1952), p. 28.

3. Robert Bolt, *A Man for All Seasons* (New York: Scholastic Book Services, 1960), p. ix.

4. Ibid., pp. 94–95.

5. Abraham Maslow, *Toward a Psychology of Being* (New York: Viking Press, 1971), p. 154.

6. Clark Moustakas, *The Authentic Teacher* (Cambridge, MA: Howard A. Doyle Printing, 1966), p. 2.

2. The First Step

1. Thomas Merton, *Contemplation in a World of Action* (New York: Image Books / Doubleday, 1973), pp. 124–25.

3. Practical Considerations

1. Edmund Colledge and Bernard McGinn, trans., *Meister Eckhart: The Essential Sermons, Commentaries, Treatises and Defense* (Mahwah, NJ: Paulist Press, 1981), pp. 257–58.

2. Thomas Merton, *The Monastic Journey* (New York: Image Books / Doubleday, 1978), p. 106.

4. The Developmental Side of the Stewardship Pattern

1. Thomas Merton, *Thoughts in Solitude* (New York: Farrar, Straus and Giroux, 1981), p. 13.

2. For examples of early stewardship and social responsibility messages, see Ezek 16:49–50, Exod 7–8, and Jer 5–26.

5. Gifts of Self As Stewardship

1. Abraham Maslow, *The Farther Reaches of Human Nature* (New York: Viking Press, 1971), p. 301.

2. Erich Fromm, *The Art of Loving* (New York: Harper and Row, 1962), pp. 22–23.

3. Thomas Merton, *The Secular Journal* (New York: Farrar, Straus and Giroux, 1977), p. 259.

4. Colledge and McGinn, p. 189.

6. The Mystic Type along the Way

1. Evelyn Underhill, *Mysticism* (New York: E. P. Dutton, 1961), p. 91.

2. During the editing of my manuscript, one of my friends suggested I mention that it is possible to be a mystic and live a conventional, urban-type life. Indeed, this is so. One friend, for

example, living in southern California, where her husband was required to remain for his aerospace job, is a perfect case in point. She has arranged her life so that she devotes each morning to quiet, meditative blocks of time. Many weekends during the year she manages to spend time at a spiritual retreat, where, along with others, she experiences the silence and solitude her spirit seems to require. In this study, however, all those who fit the mystic profile lived in solitary, rural locations, having pulled away not only emotionally from conventional life but physically, too. My guess is that those with the true mystic call who find they must live in the city or suburbs would design a lifestyle insuring their privacy.

3. Underhill, p. 262.

4. In Phillips, p. 155.

5. In Underhill, p. 86.

6. John of the Cross, *Dark Night of the Soul,* trans. and ed. E. Allison Peers (Image Books / Doubleday, 1959), pp. 81–84.

7. Meher Baba, *Life at Its Best* (New York: Harper and Row, 1957), p. 51.

8. Swami Paramananda, *Christ and Oriental Ideals* (Cohasset, MA: The Vedanta Centre, 1968), p. 119.

9. John Clarke, trans., *St. Thérèse of Lisieux: Her Last Conversations* (Washington, D.C.: ICS Publications, 1977), p. 60.

10. Franz Hartman, *The Life and Doctrines of Jacob Boehme* (New York: Macoy Publishing, 1929), pp. 60–61.

11. Lee Sannella, *Kundalini* (San Francisco: H. S. Dakin, 1978), pp. 2–4.

12. George Herbert, "A True Hymn," in *The Country Parson and the Temple,* ed. John Nelson Wall (Mahwah, NJ: Paulist Press, 1981), p. 294.

13. Brother Lawrence, *The Practice of the Presence of God* (Old Tappan, NJ: Spire Books / Fleming Revell, 1980), p. 37.

14. In Richard Maurice Bucke, *Cosmic Consciousness* (New York: E. P. Dutton, 1969), p. 78.

15. Underhill, p. 87.

16. Ibid.

17. Colledge and McGinn, pp. 199–201.

18. In Shunryu Suzuki, *Zen Mind, Beginner's Mind* (New York: Weatherhill, 1975), p. 107.

19. Ibid.

7. *Illumination and Darkness along the Mystic's Way*

1. Maslow, *Toward a Psychology of Being,* p. 99.

2. Ibid., p. 101.

3. Bucke, p. 225.

4. Phillips, p. 81.

5. Abraham Maslow, *Religions, Values and Peak Experiences* (Middlesex, UK / New York: Penguin Books, 1970), p. 27.

6. See Phil 1:9–10; Eph 1:17–19; 3:14–19.

7. Thomas Keating, Basil Pennington, and Thomas E. Clarke, *Finding Grace at the Center* (Still River, MA: St. Bede Publications, 1979), p. 44–45.

8. Thomas Merton, *Contemplation in a World of Action* (New York: Image Books / Doubleday, 1973), p. 220.

9. Ibid., p. 225.

10. Sannella, p. 64.

9. *The Look of Wholeness*

1. Ram Dass, *Journey of Awakening* (New York: Bantam Books, 1978), p. 138.

2. Robert Lindner, *Must You Conform?* (New York: Grove Press, 1956), p. 169.

3. Marsha Sinetar, "Entrepreneurs, Chaos and Creativity," *Sloan's Management Review* 26, no. 2, (Winter 1985): pp. 57–62.

10. Solitude and Silence in the Development of Wholeness

1. Max Picard, *World of Silence* (South Bend, IN: Regency / Gateway, 1953), p. 17.

2. Swami Paramananda, *Silence as Yoga* (Cohasset, MA: The Vedanta Centre, 1974), pp. 22–23.

3. William Glasser, *Positive Addiction* (New York: Harper and Row, 1976).

4. Maya Pines, "Superkids," *Psychology Today* (January 1979): n.p.

5. R. D. Laing, *The Divided Self* (London: Penguin Books, 1965), Preface.

6. Pines, n.p.

7. Abraham Zaleznik, "Managers and Leaders, Are They Different?" *Harvard Business Review* 55, no. 3 (May/June 1977): pp. 67–78.

8. Pines, n.p.

9. Fritz Perls, *Ego, Hunger and Aggression* (New York: Vintage Books, 1969), p. 179.

10. Claude Naranjo and Robert E. Ornstein, *On the Psychology of Meditation* (London: Penguin Books, 1971), pp. 8–9.

11. Keating, Pennington, and Clarke, p. 12.

12. Glasser, *Positive Addiction.*

13. Kirpal Singh, *How to Develop Receptivity* (Tilton, NH: The Sant Bani Press, 1973), pp. 11–12.

References

Benjamin, Anna S., and L. H. Hackstaff, translators. *On Free Choice of the Will*. Bobbs-Merrill Educational Publishing, 1980.

Benson, Herbert. *The Relaxation Response*. Avon Books, 1976.

Bonhoeffer, Dietrich. *The Cost of Discipleship*. Macmillan, 1963.

Campbell, Anthony. *Seven States of Consciousness*. Harper and Row, 1974.

Dass, Ram. *Journey of Awakening: A Meditator's Guidebook*. Bantam, 1978.

————. *Only Dance There Is*. Doubleday, 1974.

Delaney, Gail. *Living Your Dreams*. Harper and Row, 1981.

Glaser, William. *Positive Addiction*. Harper and Row, 1976.

Goldberg, Philip. *The Intuitive Edge*. J. P. Tarcher, 1985.

Higgins, John B. *Thomas Merton on Prayer*. Doubleday, 1978.

Howes, Elizabeth B., and Sheila Moon. *The Choice Maker*. Theosophical Publishing House, 1977.

Jones, Rufus M. *The Faith and Practice of the Quakers*. Philadelphia Yearly Meeting of the Religious Society of Friends, 1958.

Kierkegaard, Søren. *Purity of Heart*. Harper and Row, 1956.

Kunkel, Fritz. *Creation Continues*. Word Books, 1973.

Maharishi Mahesh Yogi. *Transcendental Meditation*. Allied Publishers, 1963.

Merton, Thomas. *The Way of Chuang Tzu*. New Directions, 1969.

Maslow, Abraham. *Toward a Psychology of Being*. Van Nostrand, 1968.

Overstreet, H. A. *The Mature Mind*. W. W. Norton, 1984.

Pearce, Joseph Chilton. *The Crack in the Cosmic Egg*. Pocket Books, 1973.

Progoff, Ira. *At a Journal Workshop: The Basic Text and Guide for Using the Intensive Journal Process*. Dialogue House, 1977.

Saint Teresa of Avila. *The Interior Castle*. Image Books, 1961.

Shorr, Joseph E. *Go See the Movie in Your Head*. Popular Library, 1977.

Thompson, T. K. *Stewardship in Contemporary Life*. Association Press, 1965.

————. *Stewardship in Contemporary Theology*. Association Press, 1960.

Wickes, Frances G. *The Inner World of Choice*. Harper and Row, 1976.

Wojtyla, Karol (Pope John Paul II). *Love and Responsibility*. Farrar, Straus and Giroux, 1982.

About the Author

❉

Pioneering educator Marsha Sinetar's books close the seeming gap between the material and spiritual. Her body of work is growing, yet also time-tested. Her "crossover" classics, like *Don't Call Me Old, I'm Just Awakening* and *Elegant Choices, Healing Choices*, are increasingly studied in interfaith, intergenerational settings, worldwide: church, corporate, academic, health care and counseling.

As one of America's foremost exponents of the practical value of mature spirituality, this true pathfinder lives contemplatively in the Pacific Northwest, "as quietly and simply as possible." She now shares her ideas through an educational outreach aimed at an interfaith clergy, educators, spiritual directors and other helping professionals, dedicated to showing how the contemplative tradition serves the progression and diverse expressions of a dynamic spiritual wholeness.

Please visit The Center: www.marshasinetar.com.